한국어 자습서

**Talk To Me In Korean - Level 3**

This book is based on a series of published lessons,
divided into ten levels, which are currently available
at TalkToMeInKorean.com.

## Talk To Me In Korean - Level 3

| First edition published | 2012. 12. 15. |
| Second published | 2014. 5. 30. |

| Written by | TalkToMeInKorean |
| Edited by | Kyung-hwa Sun, Stephanie Morris |
| Design by | Yoona Sun, Ji-eun Son |
| Illustration by | Kyoung-hae Kim |
| Voice Recording by | Kyeong-eun Choi, Hyunwoo Sun, Seokjin Jin |

| Published by | Language Plus (Hangulpark) |
| President | Ho-yeul Eom |
| Publisher | Tae-sang Eom |
| Editor in Chief | Yi-jun Kwon |
| Registration Date | 2000. 8. 17. |
| Registration Number | 1-2718 |
| Address | Songmin Building, 300, Jahamun ro, Jongro gu, Seoul |
| Telephone | |
| Inquiry | +82-(0)2-764-1009 |
| Order | +82-(0)2-3671-0555 |
| Fax | +82-(0)2-3671-0500 |
| Website | http://www.hangulpark.com |
| E-mail | info@langpl.com |
| ISBN | 978-89-5518-186-9  18710 |
| | 978-89-5518-183-8  (set) |

# Message from the Author

Hi, everyone. Thank you for studying Korean with the Talk To Me In Korean textbooks. Our books are designed to help you learn Korean on your own, even if you do not have the opportunity to attend classroom lessons. Whenever you have questions about any part of the book, please feel free to contact us via e-mail or any preferred social media platform. We are always there for you.

After studying and practicing with this book, you will be able to hold basic and simple conversations in Korean. Please remember, however, that learning is continuous and it is really important to supplement what you learn from this book with your own individual efforts to learn and improve. For example: looking up words you want to know and building your vocabulary, practicing your pronunciation to make it more fluid and natural, or reading/listening to/watching the Korean news, just to name a few.

The most important thing about learning a new language is to have fun doing it and never be afraid of making mistakes! Thank you.

# Contents

# LESSON 01

〰〰〰

너무

Track 01　Welcome to TalkToMeInKorean Level 3, and congratulations on making it through the first two levels of the curriculum! In Level 3, we will be reviewing and building upon what we've previously introduced through Levels 1 and 2.

In this lesson, we are looking at the word 너무. This word is used every day in Korean
[neo-mu]
with two different meanings: the original dictionary meaning and the more colloquial meaning.

Basic meaning
- 너무 = **too (much)**, **excessively**

The dictionary meaning of 너무 is "too much" or "excessively."

*Sample Sentences*

너무 커요. = It's too big.
[neo-mu keo-yo.]
너무 비싸요. = It's too expensive.
[neo-mu bi-ssa-yo.]
너무 빨라요. = It's too fast.
[neo-mu ppal-la-yo.]
너무 어려워요. = It's too difficult.
[neo-mu eo-ryeo-wo-yo.]
너무 시끄러워요. = It's too noisy.
[neo-mu si-kkeu-reo-wo-yo.]
소연 씨 너무 커요. = Soyeon, you are too tall.
[so-yeon ssi neo-mu keo-yo.]
이거 너무 비싸요. = This is too expensive.
[i-geo neo-mu bi-ssa-yo.]
말이 너무 빨라요. = (Someone) speaks too fast.
[ma-ri neo-mu ppal-la-yo.]
한국어 너무 어려워요. = The Korean language is too difficult.
[han-gu-geo neo-mu eo-ryeo-wo-yo.]
여기 너무 시끄러워요. = It's too noisy here.
[yeo-gi neo-mu si-kkeu-reo-wo-yo.]

*Colloquial usage*

- 너무 = very, quite (sometimes also used in a shortened form as 넘, but only in spoken language.)

Although the basic meaning of the word 너무 is "too much" or "excessively," in colloquial Korean, it also has the meaning of "very," "quite," or "really."

*Sample Sentences*

너무 맛있어요.
[neo-mu ma-si-sseo-yo.]
= It's really tasty.

너무 좋아요.
[neo-mu jo-a-yo.]
= It's really good.

= I'm really happy about it.

너무 잘했어요.
[neo-mu ja-rae-sseo-yo.]
= It's really well done.

= You did such a good job.

너무 멋있어요.
[neo-mu meo-si-sseo-yo.]
= It's really cool.

= It looks awesome.

이 피자 너무 맛있어요.
[i pi-ja neo-mu ma-si-sseo-yo.]
= This pizza is really tasty.

이거 너무 좋아요.
[i-geo neo-mu jo-a-yo.]
= I really like this.

석진 씨, 너무 잘했어요.
[seokjin ssi, neo-mu ja-rae-sseo-yo.]
= Seokjin, you did a really great job.

저 사람 너무 멋있어요!
[jeo sa-ram neo-mu meo-si-sseo-yo!]
= That person is really cool!

너무 used to be used only in negative contexts or sentences, but it has gradually become acceptable to use in positive contexts as well. Now, most people use 너무 in both ways.

Ex)

너무 더워요.
[neo-mu deo-wo-yo.]
= It's too hot.

= It's very hot.

너무 졸려요.
[neo-mu jol-lyeo-yo.]
= I'm too sleepy.

= I'm very sleepy.

너무 바빠요.
[neo-mu ba-ppa-yo.]
= I'm too busy.

= I'm very busy.

너무 is usually combined with adjectives but it can also be used with verbs as well.

Ex)

너무 보고 싶어요.
[neo-mu bo-go si-peo-yo.]
= I miss you/him/her/them so much.

# Sample dialogue

Track 02

A: 음악 소리가 너무 커요. 줄여 주세요.
[eu-mak so-ri-ga neo-mu keo-yo. ju-ryeo ju-se-yo.]

B: 이제 괜찮아요?
[i-je gwaen-cha-na-yo?]

A: 지금은 너무 작아요.
[ji-geu-meun neo-mu ja-ga-yo.]

*A: The music is too loud. Please turn it down.*

*B: Is it okay now?*

*A: It is too quiet now.*

# Exercises for Level 3 Lesson 1

1. What is the Korean word which means "too much" or "excessively"?

(                                                    )

2. How do you write "very" or "quite" in colloquial Korean?

(                                                    )

3. Write "It's too fast." in Korean.

(                                                    )

4. How is "It's really tasty." said in Korean?

(                                                    )

5. In Korean, write "I'm too sleepy."

(                                                    )

Check the
Answers on
p. 173

-고

Track 03    It's time to start looking at more ways to make compound sentences in Korean. You will eventually want to make more complex and longer sentences when speaking as opposed to just speaking in simple sentences.

One way to accomplish this is by making compound nouns, which are also known as "noun phrases" or "nominal phrases." Of course there are many different ways to make compound nouns depending on what you want to say, but in this lesson, we are looking at how the verb ending -고 is used.
[-go]

- 고

So what exactly does -고 do? Do you remember the conjunction, 그리고? Yes, 그리고 means "and" or "and then" in Korean, and when you use -고 after a verb stem, it
[geu-ri-go]
has the same meaning as 그리고. By using the verb ending -고 instead of ending the sentence with just one verb and then starting the next one with 그리고, you can save a lot of time and make your sentence structure more practical.

**이 책은 재미있어요. 그리고 이 책은 싸요.**
[i chae-geun jae-mi-i-sseo-yo. geu-ri-go i chae-geun ssa-yo.]
= This book is interesting. And this book is cheap.

Since you are talking about the same subject in the second sentence, you can just omit "이 책은."

→ 이 책은 재미있어요. 그리고 싸요.
= This book is interesting. And (it's) cheap.

You can make this even shorter and combine the two sentences together by saying:

→ 이 책은 재미있고 싸요.
[i chae-geun jae-mi-it-go ssa-yo.]
= This book is interesting and cheap.

> **Construction:**
> Verb stem + -고 + another verb

**Ex)**
이 책은 재미있고, 싸고, 좋아요.
[i chae-geun jae-mi-it-go, ssa-go, jo-a-yo.]
= This book is interesting, cheap, and good.

** When you make a compound sentence in English using the conjunction "and" to connect smaller sentences, you need to make the tenses of the verbs agree. However, in Korean, that's not absolutely necessary, and sometimes it sounds unnatural to try to use the same tenses for every verb, especially the future tense and the past tense. Most native Korean speakers just use the past tense or the future tense in only the final verb.

*Past tense example*

어제 친구를 만났어요.
[eo-je chin-gu-reul man-na-sseo-yo.]
= I met a friend yesterday.

그리고 영화를 봤어요.
[geu-ri-go yeong-hwa-reul bwa-sseo-yo.]
= And I saw a movie.

Let's put the two sentences above together.

어제 친구를 만났어요. 그리고 영화를 봤어요.
→  어제 친구를 만났고, 영화를 봤어요.
[eo-je chin-gu-reul man-nat-go, yeong-hwa-reul bwa-sseo-yo.]
= I met a friend yesterday and saw a movie.

However, you can also say "어제 친구를 만나고, 영화를 봤어요" with the part "만나고" in the present tense.


***Future tense example***

내일 영화를 볼 거예요.
[nae-il yeong-hwa-reul bol geo-ye-yo.]
= I will watch a movie tomorrow.


서점에 갈 거예요.
[seo-jeo-me gal geo-ye-yo.]
= I will go to a bookstore.


Let's put them together.

내일 영화를 볼 거예요. 그리고 서점에 갈 거예요.
→  내일 영화를 볼 거고, 서점에 갈 거예요.
[nae-il yeong-hwa-reul bol geo-go, seo-jeo-me gal geo-ye-yo.]
= Tomorrow, I will watch a movie, and go to a bookstore.

You can also just say "내일 영화를 보고, 서점에 갈 거예요."

Since 그리고 (or in this case, -고) has the meaning of "and after that" or "and then," using -고 is a good way of talking about things that happened or will happen in a sequence.

## Sample sentences

1. 내일은 친구 만나고, 서점에 갈 거예요.
[nae-i-reun chin-gu man-na-go, seo-jeo-me gal geo-ye-yo.]
= As for tomorrow, I'm going to meet a friend and go to a bookstore.


2. 책 읽고, 공부하고, 운동했어요.
[chaek il-kko, gong-bu-ha-go, un-dong-hae-sseo-yo.]
= I read a book, studied, and did some exercise.


3. 9월에는 한국에 가고, 10월에는 일본에 갈 거예요.
[gu-wo-re-neun han-gu-ge ga-go, si-wo-re-neun il-bo-ne gal geo-ye-yo.]
= I will go to Korea in September, and I will go to Japan in October.


4. 커피 마시고, 도너츠 먹고, 케익 먹고, 우유 마셨어요. 배불러요.
[keo-pi ma-si-go, do-neo-cheu meok-go, ke-ik meok-go, u-yu ma-syeo-sseo-yo. bae-bul-leo-yo.]
= I drank some coffee, ate a donut, ate some cake, and drank some milk. I'm full.

# Sample dialogue

Track 04

A: 석진 씨, 어제 집에 가서 뭐 했어요?
[seokjin ssi, eo-je ji-be ga-seo mwo hae-sseo-yo?]

B: 그냥 씻고 잤어요. 경은 씨는요?
[geu-nyang ssit-go ja-sseo-yo. gyeong-eun ssi-neun-yo?]

A: 저는 씻고 TV 보고, 그리고 잤어요.
[jeo-neun ssit-go ti-bi bo-go, geu-ri-go ja-sseo-yo.]

A: Seokjin, what did you do after you got home yesterday?

B: I just took a shower and slept. How about you, Kyeong-eun?

A: I took a shower, watched TV, and then went to bed.

# Exercises for Level 3 Lesson 2

1. Write "I met a friend yesterday, and saw a movie" in Korean.

\* I met a friend yesterday. = 어제 친구를 만났어요.
[eo-je chin-gu-reul man-na-sseo-yo.]
\* And I saw a movie. = 그리고 영화를 봤어요.
[geu-ri-go yeong-hwa-reul bwa-sseo-yo.]

( )

2. In Korean, write "Tomorrow, I will watch a movie, and go shopping."

\* I will watch a movie tomorrow. = 내일 영화를 볼 거예요.
[nae-il yeong-hwa-reul bol geo-ye-yo.]
\* I will go shopping. = 쇼핑하러 갈 거예요.
[syo-ping-ha-reo gal geo-ye-yo.]

( )

3. How do you say, "As for tomorrow, I'm going to meet a friend and go to a bookstore"?

\*To meet = 만나다
[man-na-da]

내일은 친구 ( ) 서점에 갈 거예요.

( )

4. How would you write, "After I got home yesterday, I ate and slept"?

\*To eat = 먹다
[meok-da]

어제 집에 가서 ( ) 잤어요.

5. Write "I read a book, studied, and did some exercise" in Korean.

\* To read = 읽다
[ik-da]
\* To study = 공부하다
[gong-bu-ha-da]
\* To do exercise = 운동하다
[un-dong-ha-da]

( )

*Check the Answers on p. 173*

# LESSON 03

~~~~~~~~

### 앞에, 뒤에, 옆에, 위에, 밑에

Let's look at how to describe the relative location of things and people.

First of all, let's go over how to ask where something or someone is. The word for "where" is 어디 and the word for "to be" is 있다. For present tense, you can ask
[eo-di]
[it-da]
"어디 있어요?", or if you want to be more accurate, you can add the location marking
[eo-di i-sseo-yo?]
particle -에 and say "어디에 있어요?"
[-e]
[eo-di-e i-sseo-yo?]

어디 있어요?
[eo-di i-sseo-yo?]
= 어디에 있어요?
[eo-di-e i-sseo-yo?]
= Where is it? / Where are you? / Where are they?

어디 있었어요?
[eo-di i-sseo-sseo-yo?]
= 어디에 있었어요?
[eo-di-e i-sseo-sseo-yo?]
= Where were you? / Where have you been?

어디 있을 거예요?
[eo-di i-sseul geo-ye-yo?]
= 어디에 있을 거예요?
[eo-di-e i-sseul geo-ye-yo?]
= Where will you be? / Where are you going to be?

In order to give a response to this question, you need to know these five one-syllable words:

**앞** = front
[ap]
**뒤** = back
[dwi]
**옆** = side
[yeop]
**위** = top
[wi]
**밑** = bottom
[mit]

To use these words with other words, you add **에**, the location marking particle, to
[-e]
them.

**앞에** = in front of
[a-pe]
**뒤에** = behind
[dwi-e]
**옆에** = beside, next to
[yeo-pe]
**위에** = over, on top of
[wi-e]
**밑에** = under, below
[mi-te]

In English, these words come BEFORE the words that they modify, but in Korean, they
come AFTER the words.

**Ex)**
**자동차** = car, automobile
[ja-dong-cha]

**자동차 앞에** = in front of the car
**자동차 뒤에** = behind the car
**자동차 옆에** = beside the car; next to the car
**자동차 위에** = on the car; on top of the car
**자동차 밑에** = under the car

Combined with **있다**:
**자동차 앞에 있어요.** = It's in front of the car.
**자동차 뒤에 있어요.** = It's behind the car.
**자동차 옆에 있어요.** = It's next to the car.
**자동차 위에 있어요.** = It's on top of the car.
**자동차 밑에 있어요.** = It's under the car.

If you remember from our previous lesson (Level 1, Lesson 18) -에 is only used with
[-e]
the status of a person or an object. When you want to express actions and behaviors
that are happening, you need to use -에서.
[-e-seo]

**Ex)**

*Q:* 친구를 어디에서 만날 거예요?
[chin-gu-reul eo-di-e-seo man-nal geo-ye-yo?]
= Where are you going to meet (your) friends?

**은행 = bank
[eu-naeng]

*A:* 은행 앞에서 만날 거예요.
[eu-naeng a-pe-seo man-nal geo-ye-yo.]
= I'm going to meet (them) in front of the bank.

*A:* 은행 뒤에서 만날 거예요.
[eu-naeng dwi-e-seo man-nal geo-ye-yo.]
= I'm going to meet (them) behind the bank.

*A:* 은행 옆에서 만날 거예요.
[eu-naeng yeo-pe-seo man-nal geo-ye-yo.]
= I'm going to meet (them) beside the bank.

*Sample Sentences*

소파 위에서 자고 있어요.
[so-pa wi-e-seo ja-go i-sseo-yo.]
= I'm sleeping on the sofa.

나무 밑에서 책을 읽고 있어요.
[na-mu mi-te-seo chae-geul il-kko i-sseo-yo.]
= I'm reading a book under the tree.

나무 뒤에 숨어 있었어요.
[na-mu dwi-e su-meo i-sseo-sseo-yo.]
= I have been hiding behind the tree.

문 앞에서 통화하고 있었어요.
[mun a-pe-seo tong-hwa-ha-go i-sseo-sseo-yo.]
= I was talking on the phone in front of the door.

# Sample dialogue

**Track 06**

A: 리모컨 어디 있어요?
[ri-mo-keon eo-di i-sseo-yo?]

B: 소파 위에 없어요?
[so-pa wi-e eop-sseo-yo?]

A: 네. 없어요. 앗, 소파 밑에 있어요!
[ne. eop-sseo-yo. at, so-pa mi-te i-sseo-yo!]

*A: Where is the remote control?*

*B: Isn't it on the couch?*

*A: No, it isn't. Oh, it's under the couch!*

# Exercises for Level 3 Lesson 3

Match the Korean words to their English equivalent.

1. 앞
[ap]

a. front

2. 위
[wi]

b. back

3. 밑
[mit]

c. side

4. 뒤
[dwi]

d. top

5. 옆
[yeop]

e. bottom

6. Write "I'm sleeping on the sofa." in Korean.

소파 ( ) 자고 있어요.

Check the
Answers on
p. 173

# LESSON 04

-(으)ㄹ까요?

Track 07

The sentence structure in this lesson is really convenient. Not only can you use
-(으)ㄹ까요 to ask someone a question like "do you want to do this with me?", but you
[-(eu)l-kka-yo]
can also use it say "I wonder what the weather will be like tomorrow" or "will it be
expensive to go to Korea?" As you can see, in English, you have to use many different
words and expressions to say these sentences, but thanks to -(으)ㄹ까요, you can say
these things and much more in Korean very easily!

## -(으)ㄹ까요?

**Usage 1 : Asking oneself a question or showing doubt about something**

**Ex)**
"I wonder what is in this bag?"
"Will he be alright?"
"Will it be hot tomorrow?"
"What will she say?"
etc.

**Usage 2 : Raising a question and attracting attention of others**

**Ex)**
"Why did this happen? What do you think, everyone?"
"What do you think life is?"
etc.

**Usage 3 : Suggesting doing something together**

**Ex)**

"What shall we do now?"

"Shall we go to the movies?"

"Do you want me to help you?"

etc.

*Q: How do you know which of these meanings it takes?*

*A: It's fairly clear and easy to see which meaning it takes when you look at the context.*

*Construction*

1. Verb stems ending with a consonant + -을까요?
[-eul-kka-yo?]

- 먹다(to eat) becomes 먹을까요?
[meok-da]                    [meo-geul-kka-yo?]

2. Verb stems ending with a vowel + -ㄹ까요?
[-l-kka-yo?]

- 보다(to see) becomes 볼까요?
[bo-da]                    [bol-kka-yo?]

3. (Exception) Verb stems ending with ㄹ + -까요?
[l + -kka-yo?]

- 팔다(to sell) becomes 팔까요?
[pal-da]                    [pal-kka-yo?]

**Ex)**

시작하다(to start) becomes 시작할까요?
[si-ja-ka-da]              [si-ja-kal-kka-yo?]

공부하다(to study) becomes 공부할까요?
[gong-bu-ha-da]          [gong-bu-hal-kka-yo?]

달리다(to run) becomes 달릴까요?
[dal-li-da]                [dal-lil-kka-yo?]

놀다(to play) becomes 놀까요?
[nol-da]                  [nol-kka-yo?]

살다(to live) becomes 살까요?
[sal-da]                  [sal-kka-yo?]

Let us clarify the core of this sentence ending. By using -ㄹ까요? or -을까요?, you are basically showing your curiosity or uncertainty. For example, in usage #1, when you are asking yourself a question and showing doubt about something, you don't know what is in that bag, so you say "저 가방 안에 뭐가 있을까요? (=I wonder what is in that [jeo ga-bang a-ne mwo-ga i-sseul-kka-yo?] bag.)" instead of saying "뭐가 있어요? (What is in that bag?)". You are not directly ask-[mwo-ga i-sseo-yo?] ing someone, but you are just expressing. You are just showing your curiosity.

Even when you are suggesting to do something together with someone, you can say this because you are not sure. Like, you don't want to see a movie with your friend, but you are not really sure, so you are asking him or her. "영화 볼까요?" You are just showing your curiosity about whether that will happen or not. So, you are suggesting to him or her. You are inviting him or her to the movies.

So, basically the bottom line is you express your curiosity or uncertainty you want to know, and the usages are divided into, on the surface, three levels.

### Sample Sentences

1. 내일 비가 올까요?
   [nae-il bi-ga ol-kka-yo?]
   = Do you think it will rain tomorrow?

   = I wonder if it will rain tomorrow.

   = Will it rain tomorrow? What do you think?

   (It CANNOT mean "shall we..." because "shall we ... rain tomorrow?" does not make sense.)

2. 내일 우리 영화 볼까요?
   [nae-il u-ri yeong-hwa bol-kka-yo?]
   = Shall we see a movie tomorrow?

   = Do you want to see a movie together tomorrow?

   (It CANNOT mean "I wonder if..." because "do you assume that we will see a movie tomorrow?" generally doesn't make sense.)

3.  이 사람은 누구일까요?
    [i sa-ra-meun nu-gu-il-kka-yo?]
    = Who do you think this person is?

    = Who is this person, I wonder?

    = I wonder who this person is.

4.  커피 마실까요? 맥주 마실까요?
    [keo-pi ma-sil-kka-yo? maek-ju ma-sil-kka-yo?]
    = Shall we drink coffee? Shall we drink beer?

    = Do you want to drink coffee or beer?

### Construction for the past tense

You can add the past tense suffix -았/었/였 right after the verb stem and before -(으)ㄹ까요 to make an assumption about a past event. Since this is in the past tense, it can ONLY be used for expressing doubt or curiosity.

### Sample Sentences

어제 했을까요?
[eo-je hae-sseul-kka-yo?]
= Do you think she did it yesterday?

누가 전화했을까요?
[nu-ga jeo-nwa-hae-sseul-kka-yo?]
= Who do you think called?

어제 Taliana가 한국에 왔을까요?
[eo-je Taliana-ga han-gu-ge wa-sseul-kka-yo?]
= Do you think Taliana came to Korea yesterday?

# Sample dialogue

**Track 08**

A: 우리 이제 갈까요?
[u-ri i-je gal-kka-yo?]

B: 밥 먹고 가요.
[bap meok-go ga-yo.]

A: 아, 그럴까요?
[a, geu-reol-kka-yo?]

*A: Shall we go now?*

*B: Let's eat first and go.*

*A: Oh, shall we?*

# Exercises for Level 3 Lesson 4

1. If 보다 means "to see," how do you say, "Shall we see?"
[bo-da]

(                                      )

2. If 팔다 means "to sell," how do you write "Shall we sell?"
[pal-da]

(                                      )

3. How do you say, "Do you think it will rain tomorrow?/ I wonder if it will rain tomorrow./ Will it rain tomorrow? What do you think?"

내일 비가 (                ) ?

4. How do you say, "Do you want to drink coffee or beer?/ Shall we drink coffee? Shall we drink beer?"

* 마시다 = to drink.
[ma-si-da]

(                                      )

5. How do you say, "Shall we see a movie tomorrow?"

(                                      )

Check the
Answers on
p. 173

# LESSON 05

≋

## 쯤, 정도, 약

Track 09

In this lesson, we look at how to say "approximately" or "about" when you talk about quantity, frequency, time, etc. There are many different ways you can say this in Korean, but the most commonly used expression is 쯤.
[jjeum]

In English, "about," "approximately," and "around" are used BEFORE nouns. However, in Korean, the word 쯤 is used AFTER nouns.

**Ex)**

1 o'clock = 한 시
[han si]
Around 1 o'clock = 한 시쯤
[han si-jjeum]

1,000 won = 천 원
[cheon won]
About 1,000 won = 천 원쯤
[cheon won-jjeum]

One month = 한 달
[han dal]
Approximately one month = 한 달쯤
[han dal-jjeum]

4 kilometers = 4킬로미터
[sa kil-lo-mi-teo]
About 4 kilometers = 4킬로미터쯤
[sa kil-lo-mi-teo-jjeum]

***Similar expressions :*** 정도, 약
[jeong-do] [yak]
Just like 쯤, 정도 is used after nouns, whereas **약** is used BEFORE nouns.

**한 달** = one month
[han dal]
**한 달쯤** = about a month
[han dal-jjeum]
**한 달 정도** = about a month
[han dal jeong-do]
**약 한 달** = about a month
[yak han dal]

\* Note that 정도 has a space before it and 쯤 does not. Sometimes people also use **약** and **쯤** together or **약** and 정도 together.

**약 한 달쯤** = about a month
[yak han dal-jjeum]
**약 한 달 정도** = about a month
[yak han dal jeong-do]

*Sample sentences*

1. 100명쯤 왔어요.
[baek-myeong-jjeum wa-sseo-yo.]
= About 100 people came.

2. 독일에서 2년쯤 살았어요.
[do-gi-re-seo i-nyeon-jjeum sa-ra-sseo-yo.]
= I lived in Germany for about two years.

3. 언제쯤 갈 거예요?
[eon-je-jjeum gal geo-ye-yo?]
= Approximately when are you going to go?

4. 내일 몇 시쯤 만날까요?
[nae-il myeot si-jjeum man-nal-kka-yo?]
= Around what time shall we meet tomorrow?

5. 다섯 시쯤 어때요?
[da-seot si-jjeum eo-ttae-yo?]
= How about around five o'clock?

# Sample dialogue

Track 10

A: 석진 씨, 어제 집에 몇 시에 갔어요?
[seok-jin ssi, eo-je ji-be myeot si-e ga-sseo-yo?]

B: 8시쯤에 갔어요. 경은 씨는요?
[yeo-deol-si-jjeu-me ga-sseo-yo. gyeong-eun ssi-neun-yo?]

A: 저도 그때쯤 갔어요.
[jeo-do geu-ttae-jjeum ga-sseo-yo.]

*A: Seokjin, what time did you go home yesterday?*

*B: I went home around 8 o'clock. How about you, Kyeong-eun?*

*A: I also went (home) around that time.*

# Exercises for Level 3 Lesson 5

1.  What is the word for "approximately" or "about" when you talk about quantity, frequency, time, etc. in Korean?

(                                        )

2. How do you say, "about a month" in Korean if "one month" is 한 달?
[han dal]

(                                        )

3. How do you say, "About when are you going to go?"

(                                        )

4. If "to meet" is 만나다 and "tomorrow" is 내일 in Korean, how do you say, "Around what time shall we meet tomorrow?"
[man-na-da] [nae-il]

(                                        )

5. "To live" is 살다 in Korean. How do you say, "I lived in Korea for about two years."?
[sal-da]

(                                        )

Check the Answers on p. 173

# *LESSON 06*

-(으)ㄹ 거예요 vs -(으)ㄹ게요

Through our previous lessons, we have learned how to use the future tense. In this lesson, we are introducing one more way of talking about a future action and looking at how the two ways of talking about the future are different.

## -(으)ㄹ 거예요 vs. -(으)ㄹ게요

If you pronounce -(으)ㄹ 거예요 very quickly, it sounds similar to -(으)ㄹ게요. Many
[-(eu)l geo-ye-yo]                                                      [-(eu)l-ge-yo]
beginner-level, and even advanced learners, mix up these two endings often, but these two sentence endings for the future are used for two distinctively different purposes.

Let's look at -(으)ㄹ 거예요 first.

-(으)ㄹ 거예요 is the most basic way to express a future plan or action. You attach to the end of a verb stem.

하다 = to do
[ha-da]
하 + -ㄹ 거예요 = 할 거예요 = I will do _____. / I am going to do _____.
                    [hal geo-ye-yo]

보내다 = to send
[bo-nae-da]
보내 + -ㄹ 거예요 = 보낼 거예요 = I will send _____. / I am going to send _____.
                        [bo-nael geo-ye-yo]

웃다 = to laugh
[ut-da]
웃 + -을 거예요 = 웃을 거예요 = I will laugh.
                  [u-seul geo-ye-yo]

With -(으)ㄹ 거예요, you are simply expressing your intention or plan for a future action, or your expectation for a future state. This is NOT related to or affected by the reaction or the request of the person you're talking to.

For example, if someone asked you about your plans for the weekend, you would say "친구들 만날 거예요" ("I'm going to meet my friends") because you are planning to
[chin-gu-deul man-nal geo-ye-yo]
meet your friends no matter what the person who asked you says.

Now let's look at -(으)ㄹ게요.

-(으) ㄹ게요 is also attached to the end of a verb stem and also expresses the future, but it focuses more on your actions or decisions AS A REACTION TO or AS A RESULT OF what the other person says or thinks.

***Let's compare the two forms***

1.
할 거예요 vs. 할게요

공부할 거예요.
[gong-bu-hal geo-ye-yo.]
= I'm going to study.

= I will study.

**Here, regardless of what the other person is saying, you were ALREADY planning to study so you will, and you are not changing your mind at all, not matter what the other person says.

**Ex)**
방해하지 마세요. 공부할 거예요.
[bang-hae-ha-ji ma-se-yo. gong-bu-hal geo-ye-yo.]
= Don't disturb me. I will study.

**공부할게요.**
[gong-bu-hal-ge-yo.]
= I will study.

= (If you say so,) I will study.

= (Since the circumstances are like this,) I will study.

= (If you don't mind,) I will study.

**Here, the other person says something to you, and it makes you think "Oh, in that case, I have to study." However, you could just say it before the other person says anything, but after you say this, you wait for the other person's reaction to see if they have anything to say.

**Ex)**

**알았어요. 공부할게요.**
[a-ra-sseo-yo. gong-bu-hal-ge-yo.]
= (After assessing the atmosphere) Okay. I will study.

2.

**갈 거예요 vs. 갈게요**

**저도 갈 거예요.**
[jeo-do gal geo-ye-yo.]
= I will go (there), too.

= I'm going to go, too.

= I'm coming along, as well.

**저도 갈게요.**
[jeo-do gal-ge-yo.]
= I will come along, too(,if you don't mind).

= (In that case,) I will go there, too.

= (OK, since you say so,) I will go, too.

So in summary, you use -(으)ㄹ게요 (instead of -(으)ㄹ 거예요) when:

1. you are changing your plan according to what the other person said.

2. you want to check what the other person thinks by saying something and seeing their reaction.

3. you decide to do something because of something the other person said.

*Sample Sentences*

1. **지금 어디예요? 지금 나갈게요.**
   [ji-geum eo-di-ye-yo? ji-geum na-gal-ge-yo.]
   = Where are you now? I will go out now.

   (+ if you don't mind/if you want me to/unless you don't want me to/what do you think about that?)

   ** Here, if you say "지금 나갈 거예요," it means that regardless of where the other person is, you were already going to go out anyway, probably to an unrelated place.

2. **저 갈게요. 안녕히 계세요.**
   [jeo gal-ge-yo. an-nyeong-hi gye-se-yo.]
   = I'm going to go. Take care.

   (+ unless you want me to stay longer/unless there's something I have to stay longer to do)

   ** Here, if you say "저 갈 거예요," it means you don't care whether the other person wants you to stay or not, you will just leave anyway. In most cases, you don't want the other person to ask you to stay, and you won't even if you are asked to.

3. **그래요? 다시 할게요.**
   [geu-rae-yo? da-si hal-ge-yo.]
   = Is that so? I'll do it again.

   ** Here, if you say "다시 할거예요," it means you were already aware of the problem and that you were going to do it again anyway.

4. **내일 4시쯤에 갈게요. 괜찮아요?**
   [nae-il ne-si-jjeu-me gal-ge-yo. gwaen-cha-na-yo?]
   = I'll be there at around 4 o'clock tomorrow. Is that alright?

   ** This implies that you want the other person to let you know what he or she thinks about you going to the place at 4 o'clock. If you don't care what the other person thinks or if going at 4 o'clock will affect the other person schedule or not, you can say "내일 4시쯤에 갈 거예요."
   [nae-il ne-si-jjeu-me gal-geo-ye-yo.]

# Sample dialogue

Track 12

A: 집에 언제 갈 거예요?
[ji-be eon-je gal geo-ye-yo?]

B: 밥 먹고 바로 갈 거예요. 석진 씨는요?
[bap meok-go ba-ro gal geo-ye-yo. seok-jin ssi-neun-yo?]

A: 저는 그냥 지금 갈게요.
[jeo-neun geu-nyang ji-geum gal-ge-yo.]

A: When are you going to go home?

B: I will go right after eating. How about you, Seokjin?

A: I will just go now.

# Exercises for Level 3 Lesson 6

1. Which of the following would you use if you want to convey the meaning of "I'm going to study./I'll study regardless of what others are thinking or planning to do."?

a. 공부할 거예요.
   [gong-bu-hal geo-ye-yo]
b. 공부할게요.
   [gong-bu-hal-ge-yo]

2. Choose the phrase which best fits the following: "I will also come along (if you don't mind.)./ (In that case,) I will go there, too./ (Okay, since you say so,) I will go, too."

a. 저도 갈 거예요.
   [jeo-do gal geo-ye-yo.]
b. 저도 갈게요.
   [jeo-do gal-ge-yo.]

3. If someone asked you about your plans for the weekend, how do you say, "I'm going to meet my friends" in Korean?

a. 친구들 만날게요.
   [chin-gu-deul man-nal-ge-yo.]
b. 친구들 만날 거예요.
   [chin-gu-deul man-nal geo-ye-yo.]

4. Write "Where are you now? I will go out now (if you don't mind/if you want me to/unless you don't want me to.)."

* 지금 = now
  [ji-geum]

(                                              )

5. Translate the following sentence into Korean: "Is that so? I'll do it again."

* 다시 = again
  [da-si]

(                                              )

Check the
Answers on
p. 173

# LESSON 07

〰〰〰

## –아/어/여서

Track 13

Back in Lesson 2 of this level, we learned about the verb ending -고, which is used to connect independent clauses or actions together to form one sentence, but the two clauses do not necessarily have a strong logical relation to each other. In this lesson, we are covering the verb ending -아/어/여+서, but this particular ending connects two or more verbs in one sentence and can show a logical relationship between the verbs.

Do you remember the two conjunctions 그리고 and 그래서 from Level 2 Lesson 3?

그리고 means "and," and 그래서 means "therefore/so."
[geu-ri-go]                    [geu-rae-seo]

The verb ending -고 has the same meaning as 그리고, and the verb ending -아/어/여+
[-go]                          [geu-ri-go]
서 is similar in meaning to 그래서.
[geu-rae-seo]

Let's look at the construction and usages of -아/어/여+서 in more detail:

> **Construction**
>
> 먹다 = to eat
> [meok-da]
> 먹 (verb stem) + 어서 = 먹어서
> [meo-geo-seo]
>
> 만들다 = to make
> [man-deul-da]
> 만들 (verb stem) + 어서 = 만들어서
> [man-deu-reo-seo]

하다 = to do
[ha-da]
하 (verb stem) + 여서 = 해서
[hae-seo]

오다 = to come
[o-da]
오 (verb stem) + 아서 = 와서
[wa-seo]

### Usages

1. Reason + -아/어/여서 + result
2. An action + -아/어/여서 + another action that takes place after the first action
3. An action + -아/어/여서 + the purpose of or the plan after the action
4. Some fixed expressions

### Usage #1 : Reason + -아/어/여서 + result

**Ex)**

비가 오다 (it rains) + 못 가다 (can't go)

→ 비가 와서 못 가요. = It's raining, so I can't go.
[bi-ga wa-seo mot ga-yo.]
→ 비가 와서 못 갔어요. = It rained, so I couldn't go.
[bi-ga wa-seo mot ga-sseo-yo.]
** Note that the tense was expressed only through the final verb.

오늘은 바빠요. (Today, I'm busy.) + 영화를 못 봐요. (I can't see the movie.)

→ 오늘은 바빠서 영화를 못 봐요.
[o-neu-reun ba-ppa-seo yeong-hwa-reul mot bwa-yo.]
= I'm busy today, so I can't see the movie.

만나다 (to meet) + 반갑다 (to be glad to see someone)

→ 만나서 반갑습니다.
[man-na-seo ban-gap-seum-ni-da]
= I met you, so I'm glad. = It's nice to meet you.

→ 만나서 반가워요.
[man-na-seo ban-ga-wo-yo]
= I'm pleased to meet you. (Less formal than the sentence above)

*Usage #2* :

**An action + -아/어/여서 + another action that takes place after the first action**

Ex)

공원에 가다 (to go to the park) + 책을 읽다 (to read a book)

→ 공원에 가서 책을 읽을 거예요.
[gong-wo-ne ga-seo chae-geul il-geul geo-ye-yo.]
= I'm going to go to the park and read a book.

** Note: This does NOT mean "I'm going to the park, so I'm going to read a book."

** Also note that the tense is expressed through the final verb here as well.

친구를 만나다 (to meet a friend) + 밥을 먹다 (to eat)

→ 친구를 만나서 밥을 먹었어요.
[chin-gu-reul man-na-seo ba-beul meo-geo-sseo-yo.]
= I met a friend and ate together.

** Note that here, this sentence COULD mean that you met a friend so you ate together,

but in most cases, it will mean that you met a friend AND THEN ate together after you met

up with him/her.

→ 친구를 만나서 밥을 먹을 거예요.
[chin-gu-reul man-na-seo ba-beul meo-geul geo-ye-yo.]
= I'm going to meet a friend and eat together.

*Usage #3* :

**An action + -아/어/여서 + the purpose of or the plan after the action.**

**Ex)**

돈을 모으다 (to save up, to save money) + 뭐 하다 (to do what)

→ 돈을 모아서 뭐 할 거예요? = What are you going
[do-neul mo-a-seo mwo hal geo-ye-yo?]
to do with the money you save up? (lit. You save up money and what will you do?)

케이크를 사다 (to buy a cake) + 친구한테 주다 (to give to a friend)

→ 케이크를 사서 친구한테 줄 거예요.
[ke-i-keu-reul sa-seo chin-gu-han-te jul geo-ye-yo.]
= I'm going to buy a cake to/and give it to a friend.

** Usage 3 is similar to Usage 2 because you are doing one thing after another, so it could

be a linear action, and it could also be a purpose.

## Usage #4 : Fixed expressions

There are some fixed expressions that basically use the same -아/어/여서 structure in
them but are not often used in other forms.

**-에 따라서** = according to ~
[-e tta-ra-seo]

> **Ex)**
>
> **계획에 따라서 진행하겠습니다**
> [gye-hoe-ge tta-ra-seo ji-naeng-ha-ge-sseum-ni-da.]
> = I'll proceed according to the plan.

**예를 들어서** = for example
[ye-reul deu-reo-seo]

> **Ex)**
>
> **예를 들어서, 이렇게 할 수 있어요.**
> [ye-reul deu-reo-seo, i-reo-ke hal su i-sseo-yo.]
> = For example, you can do it like this.

*Sample sentences*

1. 한국에 가서 뭐 할 거예요?
   [han-gu-ge ga-seo mwo hal geo-ye-yo?]
= After you go to Korea, what are you going to do?

2. 서울에 와서 좋아요.
   [seo-u-re wa-seo jo-a-yo.]
= Since I came to Seoul, I'm glad.

= I'm glad to have come to Seoul.

3. 술을 너무 많이 마셔서 머리가 아파요.
   [su-reul neo-mu ma-ni ma-syeo-seo meo-ri-ga a-pa-yo.]
= I drank too much, so my head is aching.

4. 비가 와서 집에 있었어요.
   [bi-ga wa-seo ji-be i-sseo-sseo-yo.]
= It rained, so I stayed at home.

5. 요즘에 바빠서 친구들을 못 만나요.
[yo-jeu-me ba-ppa-seo chin-gu-deu-reul mot man-na-yo.]
= These days I'm busy, so I can't meet my friends.


6. 열심히 공부해서 장학금을 받을 거예요.
[yeol-si-mi gong-bu-hae-seo jang-hak-geu-meul ba-deul geo-ye-yo.]
= I'm going to study hard so I can get (and I will get) a scholarship.


7. 한국어가 너무 재미있어서 매일 공부하고 있어요.
[han-gu-geo-ga neo-mu jae-mi-i-sseo-seo mae-il gong-bu-ha-go i-sseo-yo.]
= Korean is so much fun that I'm studying it everyday.

# Sample dialogue

Track 14

A: 짐이 너무 무거워서 힘들어요.
[ji-mi neo-mu mu-geo-wo-seo him-deu-reo-yo.]

B: 맞아요. 그리고 많이 걸어서 다리도 아파요.
[ma-ja-yo. geu-ri-go ma-ni geo-reo-seo da-ri-do a-pa-yo.]

A: 좀 쉬었다 갈까요?
[jom swi-eot-da gal-kka-yo?]

A: I am tired because the luggage is too heavy.

   B: Right. And I have a pain in my legs from walking too much.

A: Shall we take a break for a while?

# Exercises for Level 3 Lesson 7

-아/어/여+서 is a verb ending that can show logical relation between verbs. 그리고
[geu-ri-go]
means "and," and 그래서 means "therefore/so." The verb ending -고 has the same
[geu-rae-seo]                                                    [-go]
meaning as 그리고, and the verb ending -아/어/여+서 has a similar meaning as 그래서.
[geu-ri-go]                                                              [geu-rae-seo]

Please answer the following questions:

1. 하다 = to do
[ha-da]
하 (verb stem) + 여서 = (              )

2. 먹다 = to eat
[meok-da]
먹 (verb stem) + 어서 = (              )

3. 오다 = to come
[o-da]
오 (verb stem) + 아서 = (              )

Match the Korean words with their English equivalents.

4. according to ~

a. 예를 들어서
[ye-reul deu-reo-seo]

b. 재미있어서
[jae-mi-i-sseo-seo]

5. for example

c. ~에 따라서
[-e tta-ra-seo]

Check the
Answers on
p. 173

# *LESSON 08*

- 같아요

Track 15 In this lesson, we are going to look at how to say that something is similar to/like or looks similar to/like something else. (i.e. "You are like an angel," "This looks like coffee," or "You are like my teacher.")

First, let's look at how to say that something is similar to something else.

**비슷하다** = **to be similar**
[bi-seu-ta-da]
- Present tense: **비슷해요** = it is similar
[bi-seu-tae-yo]

In order to say "A is similar to B," you need to use a particle that means "with" or "together with." Do you remember which particle that is? It's -랑 or -하고. (Go back to Level 2 Lesson 4 to review!)

A랑 **비슷해요**. = It's similar to A.
[A-rang bi-seu-tae-yo.]
B하고 **비슷해요**. = It's similar to B.
[B-ha-go bi-seu-tae-yo.]

> **Ex)**
> 도쿄는 서울하고 비슷해요? = Is Tokyo similar to Seoul?
> [do-kyo-neun seo-u-ra-go bi-seu-tae-yo?]
> 참외는 멜론하고 비슷해요. = 참외 (a type of fruit) is similar to melon.
> [cha-moe-neun mel-lo-na-go bi-seu-tae-yo.]

Now, let's look at the word for "to be the same" in Korean.

같다 = to be the same
[gat-da]
- Present tense: 같아요 = it's the same, they are the same
[ga-ta-yo]

In English, when you want to say that A is the same as B, you use the word "as", but in Korean, we still use -랑 or -하고.

A랑 같아요. = It's the same as A.
[A-rang ga-ta-yo.]
A하고 B는 같아요. = A and B are the same.
[A-ha-go B-neun ga-ta-yo.]

### Ex)

이거랑 이거랑 같아요? = Is this the same as this?/ Are these two things the same?
[i-geo-rang i-geo-rang ga-ta-yo?]
우리는 나이가 같아요. = We have the same age. (lit. "For us, the age is the same.")
[u-ri-neun na-i-ga ga-ta-yo.]

Now you know how to use -랑/-하고 비슷하다 and -랑/-하고 같다 to express that something is similar to or the same as something else in Korean!

However, if you use the word 같다, which means "to be the same," without the particle -랑 or -하고, it has a different meaning.
[gat-da]

### Construction
**Noun** + 같다 = to be like + Noun / to look like + Noun / to seem to be + Noun

### Ex)

커피 같아요. = It's like coffee. / It seems to be coffee. / It looks like coffee.
[keo-pi ga-ta-yo]
거짓말 같아요. = It seems to be a lie. / It sounds like a lie.
[geo-jit-mal ga-ta-yo]
로봇 같아요. = It's like a robot. / It seems to be a robot. / It looks like a robot.
[ro-bot ga-ta-yo]

*Sample sentences*

1. 저 사람은 로봇 같아요.
[jeo sa-ra-meun ro-bot ga-ta-yo.]
= That person is like a robot.

2. 경은 씨는 천사 같아요.
[gyeong-eun ssi-neun cheon-sa ga-ta-yo.]
= Kyeong-eun is like an angel.

3. 현우 씨는 천재 같아요.
[hyeo-nu ssi-neun cheon-jae ga-ta-yo.]
= Hyunwoo seems to be a genius.

4. 그 이야기는 거짓말 같아요.
[geu i-ya-gi-neun geo-jit-mal ga-ta-yo.]
= That story sounds like a lie.

5. 이 강아지는 고양이 같아요.
[i gang-a-ji-neun go-yang-i ga-ta-yo.]
= This puppy is like a cat.

In this lesson, we looked at how to use 같아요 with nouns only, but in the next lesson, we'll build upon your knowledge and learn how to use 같아요 with verbs and say many more things!

# Sample dialogue

**Track 16**

A: 오늘 너무 더워서 여름 같아요.
[o-neul neo-mu deo-wo-seo yeo-reum ga-ta-yo.]

B: 맞아요. 어제까지는 추워서 겨울 같았는데.
[ma-ja-yo. eo-je-kka-ji-neun chu-wo-seo gyeo-ul ga-tan-neun-de.]

A: 요즘 날씨가 정말 이상해요.
[yo-jeum nal-ssi-ga jeong-mal i-sang-hae-yo.]

*A: It's so hot today, so it feels like summer.*

*B: That's right. Until yesterday, it was cold so it felt like winter.*

*A: The weather is weird these days.*

# Exercises for Level 3 Lesson 8

1. What is "to be similar" in Korean?

(                                        )

2. Write "We are the same age" in Korean.
* 같다 = to be the same
  [gat-da]

(                                        )

3. Translate the following sentence to Korean: "Is this the same as this?"

(                                        )

4. Write "It's like coffee. / It seems to be coffee. / It looks like coffee." in Korean.

(                                        )

5. Write "That story sounds like a lie." in Korean.
* 거짓말 = a lie
  [geo-jit-mal]

(                                        )

Check the
Answers on
p. 173-174

# LESSON 09

-(으)ㄴ/는/(으)ㄹ 것 같아요

Track 17 In the previous lesson, we looked at how to use 같아요 after nouns to mean "it looks
[ga-ta-yo]
like" or "it seems to be" something.

**Ex)**

커피 같아요. = It looks like coffee. / I think it's coffee.
[keo-pi ga-ta-yo.]
저 사람 소연 씨 같아요. = That person looks like So-yeon. / I think that person is
[jeo sa-ram so-yeon ssi ga-ta-yo.]
So-yeon.

In the examples above, both 커피 and 소연 씨 are nouns, so as you can see, it is rela-
tively simple to use 같아요 in the sentences. All you have to do is add 같아요 after the
nouns.

However, when you want to use 같아요 with verbs, you'll first need to change the
verb into its noun form. There are a few different ways to change a verb into a noun,
but here, we are going to use the -ㄴ 것 form. We learned about this noun form in
Level 2 Lesson 19.

Let's review a little bit:

1. Descriptive verbs
   Verb stem + -(으)ㄴ 것

   **Ex)**

   예쁘다 = to be pretty
   [ye-ppeu-da]

예쁜 것 = being pretty; something pretty; the thing that is pretty
[ye-ppeun geot]

2. Action verbs

[Present tense] Verb stem + -는 것

**Ex)**
말하다 = to talk, to speak; to say
[ma-ra-da]
말하는 것 = talking; what one is saying; the act of talking
[ma-ra-neun geot]

[Past tense] Verb stem + -(으)ㄴ 것

**Ex)**
말한 것 = what one said; the fact that one talked
[ma-ran geot]

[Future tense] Verb stem + -(으)ㄹ 것

**Ex)**
말할 것 = what one will say; the fact that one will talk
[ma-ral geot]

### *How to use 같아요 with verbs*

Now that we've reviewed how to change verbs into the -ㄴ 것 noun form, we are almost there! Since you already have the verbs in the noun forms, you just have to add 같아요 after 것. It's the same as when you use 같아요 with nouns.

-(으)ㄴ 것 같아요 = present tense for descriptive verbs / past tense for action verbs
-는 것 같아요 = present tense for action verbs
-(으)ㄹ 것 같아요 = future tense for action/descriptive verbs

***What does -것 같아요 mean?***

Even when 같아요 is combined with verbs, since the -것 part already makes them nouns, the basic meanings and usages are the same as "Noun + 같아요."

1. "It looks like..."
3. "To me it looks like..."
5. "I think it will..."

2. "It seems to be..."
4. "I think it is..."
6. "I think it was...." etc.

**Ex)**

이상하다 = to be strange
[i-sang-ha-da]
이상하 + ㄴ 것 같아요 = 이상한 것 같아요.

= It seems to be strange. / I think it's strange.

눈이 오다 = to snow
[nu-ni o-da]
눈이 오 + 는 것 같아요 = 눈이 오는 것 같아요.

= It seems to be snowing. / I think it's snowing.

눈이 오 + ㄹ 것 같아요 = 눈이 올 것 같아요.

= I think it will snow. / It seems like it will snow.

이야기하다 = to tell; to talk
[i-ya-gi-ha-da]
이야기하 + ㄴ 것 같아요 = 이야기한 것 같아요.

= I think they told them. / It looks like they talked.

이야기하 + ㄹ 것 같아요 = 이야기할 것 같아요.

= I think they will talk. / It seems like they will talk.

이야기하 + 는 것 같아요 = 이야기하는 것 같아요.

= I think they are talking. / They seem to talk to each other.

As you can see from the examples above, when you want to say "I think" in Korean, you can use 것 같아요.

*Sample sentences*

1. 여기 비싼 것 같아요.
   [yeo-gi bi-ssan geot ga-ta-yo.]
   = I think this place is expensive.

   = This place looks expensive.

   = This place seems to be expensive.

2. 그런 것 같아요.
   [geu-reon geot ga-ta-yo.]
   = I think so.

   = It seems to be so.

   = It looks like it.

   ** Verb = 그렇다 (irregular) = to be so; to be that way

3. 이 영화 재미있을 것 같아요.
   [i yeong-hwa jae-mi-i-sseul geot ga-ta-yo]
   = I think this movie will be interesting.

   = This movie looks like it will be interesting (to watch).

4. 이 가방, 여기에서 산 것 같아요.
   [i ga-bang, yeo-gi-e-seo san geot ga-ta-yo.]
   = This bag seems like we bought it here.

   = I think I bought this bag here.

5. 아마 안 할 것 같아요.
   [a-ma an hal geot ga-ta-yo.]
   = I think I probably won't do it.

   = It looks like we are probably not going to do it.

# Sample dialogue

Track 18

A: 이 우유, 맛이 조금 이상한 것 같아요.
[i u-yu, ma-si jo-geum i-sang-han geot ga-ta-yo.]

B: 그래요?
[geu-rae-yo?]

A: 네. 상한 것 같아요.
[ne. sang-han geot ga-ta-yo.]

*A: This milk, I think it tastes a bit strange.*

*B: Does it?*

*A: Yes. I think it's gone bad.*

# Exercises for Level 3 Lesson 9

"To tell" or "to talk" is **이야기하다** in Korean.
[i-ya-gi-ha-da]

Match the English sentence with its Korean equivalent.

1. I think they told them. /
   It looks like they talked.

    a. **이야기할 것 같아요.**
    [i-ya-gi-hal geot ga-ta-yo.]

2. I think they are talking. /
   They seem to talk to each other.

    b. **이야기한 것 같아요.**
    [i-ya-gi-han geot ga-ta-yo.]

    c. **이야기하는 것 같아요.**
    [i-ya-gi-ha-neun geot ga-ta-yo.]

3. I think they will talk. /
   It seems like they will talk.

4. Write "I think this place is expensive./ It looks expensive./ This place seems to be expensive." in Korean.

* To be expensive = **비싸다**
[bi-ssa-da]

(                                            )

5. Translate the following to Korean: "I think so./ It seems to be so./It looks like it."

* To be so; to be that way = **그렇다**
[geu-reo-ta]

(                                            )

*Check the Answers on p. 174*

# LESSON 10

## -기 전에

Track 19

In this lesson, we are going to learn how to say "before -ing" in Korean. As with many Korean expressions and prepositions, the order is the opposite from English. In English, the word "before" goes before the clause or the word, but in Korean, it goes after.

The key syllable here is **전**. The Chinese character for **전** is 前 and it means "before," "front," or "earlier". To this noun, you add the particle -**에** to make it a preposition.
[jeon]                                                                                                          [-e]

**전에** = before (+ noun)

**수업 전에** = before class
[su-eop jeo-ne]
**일요일 전에** = before Sunday
[i-ryo-il jeo-ne]
**1시 전에** = before 1 o'clock
[han-si jeo-ne]

Since **전에** is used after nouns, in order to use it with verbs such as "going" or "leaving", you need to change the verbs into nouns.

In our previous lesson, to use verbs before **같다**, we changed the verbs into the -**ㄴ 것**
[gat-da]
form. In this case, however, you need to change verbs into the -**기** form, the first of
[-gi]
the verbal noun forms that we learned in one of our previous lessons.

가다 → 가기 (going)　　　　　→ 가기 전에 = before going
[ga-da]　[ga-gi]

사다 → 사기 (buying)　+ 전에　→ 사기 전에 = before buying
[sa-da]　[sa-gi]

먹다 → 먹기 (eating)　　　　　→ 먹기 전에 = before eating
[meok-da]　[meok-gi]

**Ex)**

집에 가다 = to go home
[ji-be ga-da]
→ 집에 가기 전에

　　= before going home; before you go home

공부하다 = to study
[gong-bu-ha-da]
→ 공부하기 전에

　　= before studying; before you study

돈을 내다 = to pay money
[do-neul nae-da]
→ 돈을 내기 전에

　　= before paying money; before you pay money

*Sample sentences*

1. 여기 오기 전에 뭐 했어요?
[yeo-gi o-gi jeo-ne mwo hae-sseo-yo?]
= What were you doing before you came here?

2. 집에 가기 전에 술 마실 거예요.
[ji-be ga-gi jeo-ne sul ma-sil geo-ye-yo.]
= I'm going to drink before I go home.

** 집에 가다 = to go back home

3. 들어오기 전에 노크하세요.
[deu-reo-o-gi jeo-ne no-keu-ha-se-yo.]
= Knock before you come in.

** 들어오다 = to come in

4. 사기 전에 잘 생각하세요.
[sa-gi jeo-ne jal saeng-ga-ka-se-yo.]
= Think well before you buy it.

** 사다 = to buy


5. 도망가기 전에 잡으세요.
[do-mang-ga-gi jeo-ne ja-beu-se-yo.]
= Catch him before he runs away.

** 도망가다 = to run away

# Sample dialogue

Track 20

A: 경은 씨, 우리 수영장 가기 전에 밥부터 먹을까요?
[gyeong-eun ssi, u-ri su-yeong-jang ga-gi jeo-ne bap-bu-teo meo-geul-kka-yo?]

B: 운동하기 바로 전에 밥 먹으면 안 좋아요.
[un-dong-ha-gi ba-ro jeo-ne bap meo-geu-myeon an jo-a-yo.]

A: 아, 그래요? 그럼 끝나고 먹어요.
[a, geu-rae-yo? geu-reom kkeun-na-go meo-geo-yo.]

*A: Kyeong-eun, shall we eat first before going to the swimming pool?*

*B: Eating right before exercising is not good.*

*A: Ah, it isn't? Then let's eat after (swimming).*

# Exercises for Level 3 Lesson 10

1. How do you write "before (+noun)" in Korean?

(                                                          )

2. Write "before studying; before you study" in Korean.

(                                                          )

3.  Write "before paying money; before you pay money" in Korean.

* To pay money = 돈을 내다
  [do-neul nae-da]

(                                                          )

4. Translate the following sentence to Korean: "Knock before you come in."

* 들어오다 = to come in
  [deu-reo-o-da]

(                                                          )

5. Write "Think well before you buy." in Korean.

* To buy = 사다
  [sa-da]

(                                                          )

Check the
Answers on
p. 174

*Places in Korea*
# Daehakro (대학로)

대학로 *(Dae-hak-ro) means "college street", and it's actually pronounced* 대항노
*(dae-hang-no), which is slightly different than the "official" romanization. This is
because of a tricky little Hangul pronunciation rule:*
*When the letter "ㄱ" is the* 받침 *(final consonant) and is followed by "ㄹ," the "ㄱ"
is changed to "ㅇ" and "ㄹ" becomes "ㄴ."*
*This is mostly for ease of pronunciation because it's WAY easier to say* 대항노
*than it is to try and spit out* 대학로 *at native speed. Plus, no one will know what
you're talking about if you pronounce it as "dae-hak-ro."*
*Some other examples of this rule are:*

독립 (independence) → 동닙
석류 (pomegranate tree) → 성뉴
목련 (magnolia) → 몽년

It may seem a little confusing at first, but once you start practicing, you'll find that it just naturally comes out this way.

Anyway, now that we have that out of the way, let's learn more about 대학로!

대학로 used to be the main road that bordered Seoul National University's College of Arts and Sciences. Although that campus moved to another part of the city some time ago, 대학로 is still the core of about a half dozen major university branches. It's also known as the "street of youth, art, and freedom", and from this name, it may seem that only younger people frequent the streets of 대학로. That is certainly not the case. 대학로 is more of an intersection where the youth of today and the youth of half a generation ago meet to explore and share what is quintessentially Korea: tradition and modernity.

One of the best spots to experience this generational crossroads is 마로니에 공원 (Marronnier Park). 마로니에 공원 used to be the spot of Seoul National University's College of Arts and Sciences campus, but has since become a terrific cultural space. At the center of 마로니에 공원 is a symbolic 밤나무 (Marronnier/ Chestnut tree), and surrounding it are dozens of sculptures and art centers. This place is particularly good for hanging out on the weekends because of the numerous bands, singers, comedians, and dance troupes that gather here to give performances. You may also run into a few street artists that will draw your picture for a small price, or a fortuneteller that may unveil your future :D

This area is famous for being a "theater district" since there is a high concentration of theaters and concert halls. If you like comedy, you can find live comedy shows here, too. The most famous one is the live version of KBS's famous comedy show, "Gag Concert." How's that for famous? At any rate, you can find posters for various productions hanging up all over the streets of 대학로, and

*this is definitely one of the best places in Seoul to experience plays and musicals that sometimes aren't huge productions or very expensive.*

*Although 대학로 is more of a theater district, there are a good number of international restaurants, cafes, cinemas, a jazz bar, and some small stores to shop at. Since it's a college area, everything is really cheap compared to some other places in the city. Whether you're looking to try some traditional Korean liquor, known as 막걸리, and 파전 (Korean pancake) with your friends, or purchasing some skin care products, you will definitely get your money's worth at 대학로!*

*With Former Prime Minister Chang Myeon's house, the Hyehwa-dong Residence Center, the first president of Korea's former residence, and a number of other cultural experiences, 대학로 also has a lot of history behind it. It's also just a stone's throw away from 낙산 (Naksan), the Seoul Fortress Wall, and 동대문, a.k.a. The Great East Gate, which makes it a SUPER good place to start exploring Seoul.*

*This blog post just scratched the surface of all that 대학로 has to offer, so make sure to get your happy little self over here to experience it first-hand.*

\*\*\*

**Thanks for reading and
good luck with the rest of Level 3!**

# LESSON 11

ㅂ 불규칙

Track 21 You have learned a lot about Korean verbs so far - conjugations, rules, etc. Let's continue our verb learning journey with irregularities! Just like many other languages, Korean has some irregularities which, over the course of time, were used more and more, so they eventually became a fixed rule.

Korean has much fewer verb irregularities than some other languages, but you will encounter these irregularities everywhere as you learn and speak Korean. We would like to introduce one of these irregularities in this lesson.

ㅂ-irregular

This means that if verbs have ㅂ at the end of their verb stems, and they are followed by a suffix that starts with a vowel, the ㅂ part will change to 오 or 우.

> If the vowel before ㅂ is 오, you change ㅂ to 오.
> If the vowel before ㅂ is not 오, you change ㅂ to 우.

**Ex)**
돕다 = to help
[dop-da]
= 도 + ㅂ + 다 → 도 + 오 + 아요 = 도와요
** Note that it is NOT 돕아요
[present tense] 도와요   [past tense] 도왔어요   [future tense] 도울 거예요
        [do-wa-yo]          [do-wa-sseo-yo]              [do-ul geo-ye-yo]

**어렵다** = to be difficult
[eo-ryeop-da]
= 어려 + ㅂ + 다 → 어려 + 우 + 어요. = 어려워요.

[present tense] 어려워요     [past tense] 어려웠어요     [future tense] 어려울 거예요
           [eo-ryeo-wo-yo]              [eo-ryeo-wo-sseo-yo]                    [eo-ryeo-ul geo-ye-yo]

**춥다** = to be cold → 추 + 우 + 어요 = 추워요.
[chup-da]
[present tense] 추워요     [past tense] 추웠어요     [future tense] 추울 거예요
           [chu-wo-yo]              [chu-wo-sseo-yo]                    [chu-wo-sseo-yo]

### Some other irregular words

**눕다** = to lie down → **누워요.**
[nup-da]                    [nu-wo-yo.]
**굽다** = to bake → **구워요.**
[gup-da]              [gu-wo-yo.]
**덥다** = to be hot (weather) → **더워요.**
[deop-da]                        [deo-wo-yo.]
**쉽다** = to be easy → **쉬워요.**
[swip-da]                [swi-wo-yo.]
**맵다** = to be spicy → **매워요.**
[meap-da]                 [mae-wo-yo.]
**귀엽다** = to be cute → **귀여워요.**
[gwi-yeop-da]               [gwi-yeo-wo-yo.]
**밉다** = to hate; to be dislikeable → **미워요.**
[mip-da]                                [mi-wo-yo.]
**아름답다** = to be beautiful → **아름다워요.**
[a-reum-dap-da]                     [a-reum-da-wo-yo.]

Remember that these verbs have irregular forms ONLY WHEN the suffix following the verb stem starts with a VOWEL. So, if you have suffixes like -는 or -고, they still keep the ㅂ.

### Ex)
**돕다** = to help → 돕 + -는 것 = 돕는 것
[dop-da]

### Irregularities in irregular verbs

Although the ㅂ irregular rule is applied to most verbs that have ㅂ in them, some verbs do not follow this rule.

Action verbs:

- **입다** = to wear
  [ip-da]
- **잡다** = to catch
  [jap-da]
- **씹다** = to bite
  [ssip-da]

Descriptive verbs:

- **좁다** = to be narrow
  [job-da]
- **넓다** = to be wide
  [neol-tta]

These words still keep their ㅂ in front of vowels.

> **Ex)**
>
> 입다 → 입어요 (Not 이워요)
>
> 좁다 → 좁아요 (Not 조아요)

*Sample sentences*

1. 이 문제는 어려워요.
[i mun-je-neun eo-ryeo-wo-yo.]
= This problem is difficult.

2. 이거 너무 귀여워요.
[i-geo neo-mu gwi-yeo-wo-yo.]
= This is so cute.

3. 서울은 겨울에 정말 추워요.
[seo-u-reun gyeo-eu-re jeong-mal chu-wo-yo.]
= In Seoul, it's really cold in the winter.

4. TTMIK에서 공부하면, 한국어 공부가 쉬워요.
[TTMIK-e-seo gong-bu-ha-myeon, han-gu-geo gong-bu-ga swi-wo-yo.]
= If you study at TTMIK, studying Korean is easy.

# Sample dialogue

**Track 22**

A: 현우 씨, 왜 누워 있어요?
[hyeo-nu ssi, wae nu-wo i-sseo-yo?]

B: 너무 더워서요.
[neo-mu deo-wo-seo-yo.]

A: 누워 있으면 안 더워요?
[nu-wo i-sseu-myeon an deo-wo-yo?]

B: 네. 소파가 차가워서요.
[ne. so-pa-ga cha-ga-wo-seo-yo.]

*A: Hyunwoo, why are you lying down?*

*B: Because it's too hot.*

*A: It's not hot when you are lying down?*

*B: No, because the couch is cold.*

# Exercises for Level 3 Lesson 11

1. Since the ㅂ in the verb 돕다 (to help) is irregular, it changes to 도와요. Not all verbs
[dop-da]                                                    [do-wa-yo]
have an irregular ㅂ, so choose the verb from the list below which does not have a
ㅂ-irregular:

1) 입다 = to wear
[ip-da]
2) 눕다 = to lie down
[nup-da]
3) 춥다 = to be cold
[chup-da]
4) 쉽다 = to be easy
[swip-da]

2. "To be difficult" is "어렵다" in Korean. Present tense for "어렵다" is "어려워요".
[eo-ryeop-da]                                [eo-ryeop-da]     [eo-ryeo-wo-yo]
What's the past tense form?

1) 어려울 거예요
[eo-ryeo-ul geo-ye-yo]
2) 어려웠어요
[eo-ryeo-wo-sseo-yo]

Write following sentences in Korean:
3. This is so cute!

* 귀엽다 = to be cute
[gwi-yeop-da]

(                                                    )

4. This problem is difficult.

* 어렵다 = to be difficult
[eo-ryeop-da]

(                                                    )

5. In Seoul, it's really cold in the winter.

* 춥다 = to be cold
[chup-da]

(                                                    )

Check the
Answers on
p. 174

# LESSON 12
〰〰〰

그래도

Track 23   We have introduced a few different conjunctions so far through our previous lessons, and today we have one more interesting conjunction to introduce.

The word is 그래도.

(In Level 2 Lesson 3, we introduced 그래서, which means "so", "therefore", and
[geu-rae-seo]
그래도 is only different at the end.)
[geu-rae-do]

그래도 means "but still," "however," "nonetheless," or "nevertheless"

### Ex)
비가 와요. 그래도 갈 거예요?
[bi-ga wa-yo. geu-rae-do gal geo-ye-yo?]
= It's raining. Are you still going?

Let's break it down:
그래도 = 그래 + 도
- 그래 = 그렇게 해 or 그렇게 하여(to do it in such a way, to do that)
- 도 = also, too, even

The literal meaning of "그래 + 도" is "even if you do that," "even if that happens," or "if you do that too" with the meaning of "still" added to its context.

*Sample sentences*

1. 한국어는 어려워요. 그래도 재미있어요.
[han-gu-geo-neun eo-ryeo-wo-yo. geu-rae-do jae-mi-i-sseo-yo.]
= Korean is difficult. But still, it is interesting.


2. 어제는 비가 왔어요. 그래도 축구를 했어요.
[eo-je-neun bi-ga wa-sseo-yo. geu-rae-do chuk-gu-reul hae-sseo-yo.]
= Yesterday, it rained. Nevertheless, we played soccer.


3. 저도 돈이 없어요. 그래도 걱정하지 마세요.
[jeo-do do-ni eop-sseo-yo. geu-rae-do geok-jeong-ha-ji ma-se-yo.]
= I don't have money, either. But still, don't worry.


4. 노래방에 가야 돼요. 그래도 노래 안 할 거예요.
[no-rae-bang-e ga-ya dwae-yo. geu-rae-do no-rae an hal geo-ye-yo.]
= I have to go to a 노래방. However, I'm not going to sing.


5. 요즘 바빠요. 그래도 한국어를 공부하고 있어요.
[yo-jeum ba-ppa-yo. geu-rae-do han-gu-geo-reul gong-bu-ha-go i-sseo-yo.]
= I'm busy these days. But I'm still studying Korean.


Sometimes when you are talking with your friends, you don't want to finish your sentence, and you just want to say "but still, come on...," you can just say "그래도" as an interjection. Iif you want to be more polite, or if you want to make sure that you are not being rude, you can add -요 to the end and say "그래도요." However, since "도 요" takes a bit of work to pronounce, some people in Seoul, especially girls, say "그래 두요" instead of "그래도요."

# Sample Dialogue

Track 24

A: 저는 더운 날씨가 너무 싫어요.
[jeo-neun deo-un nal-ssi-ga neo-mu si-reo-yo.]

B: 그래도, 저는 여름이 좋아요.
[geu-rae-do, jeo-neun yeo-reu-mi jo-a-yo.]

A: 여름에 너무 덥지 않아요?
[yeo-reu-me neo-mu deop-ji a-na-yo?]

B: 더워요. 그래도 저는 여름이 좋아요.
[deo-wo-yo. geu-rae-do jeo-neun yeo-reu-mi jo-a-yo.]

A: I really hate the hot weather.

B: But still, I like summer.

A: Isn't it too hot in summer?

B: It's hot, but I still like it.

# Exercises for Level 3 Lesson 12

1. How do you say "but still," "however," or "nonetheless" in Korean?

(                                                    )

Fill in the blanks with the appropriate Korean word to complete the sentence.

2. 노래방에 가야 돼요. (      ) 노래 안 할 거예요.
= I have to go to a 노래방 (singing room). But still, I'm not going to sing.

(                                                    )

3. 어제는 (                ). (         ) 축구를 했어요.
= Yesterday, it rained. But still, we played soccer.
* To play soccer = 축구를 하다
  [chuk-gu-reul ha-da]

4. 한국어는 (          ). (          ) 재미있어요.
= Korean is difficult. But still, it's interesting.
* To be interesting = 재미있다
  [jae-mi-it-da]

*Check the Answers on p. 174*

# LESSON 13

## descriptive verbs + - ㄴ + 명사

Track 25

Korean and English are different in many ways, but one of the key differences is that in Korean, "adjectives" also have a verb form. For example, if you say "beautiful" in English, it is an adjective and you can look it up in the dictionary in that way. In Korean, however, you can only find 예쁘다 in the dictionary, which is in the verb
[ye-ppeu-da]
form and means "to be beautiful." You cannot find 예쁜, the adjective form of 예쁘다
[ye-ppeun]
(beautiful), in the dictionary.

Therefore, all the adjectives in English have to be in the "to be + adjective" form in order to mean the same thing as the Korean descriptive verbs.

**Ex)**

싸다 → It does NOT mean "cheap," it means "to be cheap."
[ssa-da]
바쁘다 → It does NOT mean "busy," it means "to be busy".
[ba-ppeu-da]
맛있다 → It does NOT mean "delicious," it means "to be delicious."
[ma-sit-da]

Since the "adjectives" are presented in the form of "descriptive verbs" in Korean, you can conjugate them just like other "action verbs" whereas the adjectives never change forms.

For example, if you say "It is fun," "It was fun," or "It will be fun" in English, the word "fun" does not change its form. But in Korean, since the descriptive verbs are conjugated, you change 재미있다 to 재미있어요(present tense), 재미있었어요(past tense),
[jae-mi-it-da]   [jae-mi-i-sseo-yo]                        [jae-mi-i-sseo-sseo-yo]
and 재미있을 거예요(future tense).
[jae-mi-i-sseul geo-ye-yo]

### *What if you want to use them as adjectives?*

Good question. When you want to use descriptive verbs in the adjective form, you need to change them to the -(으)ㄴ form.

> - **Verb stems ending with a vowel + -ㄴ**
> - **Verb stems ending with a consonant + -은**

**Ex)**

작다 = to be small
[jak-da]
→ 작 + -은 = 작은 = small
      [ja-geun]
→ 작은 집 = a small house
   [ja-geun jip]

빠르다 = to be fast
[ppa-reu-da]
→ 빠르 + -ㄴ = 빠른 = fast
      [ppa-reun]
→ 빠른 차 = a fast car
   [ppa-reun cha]

조용하다 = to be quiet
[jo-yong-ha-da]
→ 조용하 + -ㄴ = 조용한 = quiet
      [jo-yong-han]
→ 조용한 방 = a quiet room
   [jo-yong-han bang]

비싸다 = to be expensive
[bi-ssa-da]
→ 비싸 + -ㄴ = 비싼 = expensive
      [bi-ssan]
→ 비싼 컴퓨터
   [bi-ssan keom-pyu-teo]

Exceptions

하얗다 → 하얀 = white [NOT 하얗은]
      [ha-yan]
그렇다 → 그런 = such [NOT 그렇은]
      [geu-reon]
달다 → 단 = sweet [NOT 달은]
      [dan]

*Common Mistake*

Many people make the mistake of trying to say "to be (이에요)" + "adjective" just like in English.

예쁜이에요 ( x )
비싼이에요 ( x )

This is incorrect. Since all "adjectives" in Korean are "descriptive verbs," you need to conjugate them like verbs:

예쁘다 → 예뻐요 ( o )
비싸다 → 비싸요 ( o )

*Sample sentences*

1. 좋은 아이디어예요.
   [jo-eun a-i-di-eo-ye-yo.]
   = It's a good idea.

2. 이상한 사람이에요.
   [i-sang-han sa-ra-mi-e-yo.]
   = He's a strange person.

3. 더 작은 가방 있어요?
   [deo ja-geun ga-bang i-sseo-yo?]
   = Do you have a smaller bag?

4. 차가운 커피 마시고 싶어요.
   [cha-ga-un keo-pi ma-si-go si-peo-yo.]
   = I want to drink some cold coffee.

5. 나쁜 사람이에요.
   [na-ppeun sa-ra-mi-e-yo]
   = He is a bad person.

# Sample dialogue

Track 26

A: 경은 씨, 매운 음식 좋아해요?
[gyeong-eun ssi, mae-un eum-sik jo-a-hae-yo?]

B: 네, 좋아해요. 현우 씨는요?
[ne, jo-a-hae-yo. hyeo-nu ssi-neun-yo?]

A: 저는 다 좋아해요. 느끼한 음식도 좋아해요.
[jeo-neun da jo-a-hae-yo. neu-kki-han eum-sik-do jo-a-hae-yo.]

B: 아, 저는 느끼한 음식은 안 좋아해요.
[a, jeo-neun neu-kki-han eum-si-geun an jo-a-hae-yo.]

A: Kyeong-eun, do you like spicy food?

B: Yes, I do. How about you Hyunwoo?

A: I like all kinds of food. I even like greasy food.

B: Oh, I don't like greasy food.

# Exercises for Level 3 Lesson 13

When you want to use descriptive verbs in the adjective form, you need to change them to the -(으)ㄴ form.

Please change the descriptive verbs into the adjective form.

1. 작다 = to be small → (          ) = small
   [jak-da]

2. 비싸다 = to be expensive → (          ) = expensive
   [bi-ssa-da]

3. 하얗다 = to be white → (          ) = white
   [ha-yat-ta]

4. 달다 = to be sweet → (          ) = sweet
   [dal-da]

5. "To be big" is 크다 in Korean. How do you say, "Do you have a bigger bag?"
   [keu-da]

(                                                    )

Check the
Answers on
p. 174

# LESSON 14

action verbs + -는/(으)ㄴ/(으)ㄹ + 명사

Track 27

In the previous lesson, we looked at how to conjugate descriptive verbs to make adjectives in Korean. You are now familiar with the fact that Korean and English have different systems when it comes to using adjectives. But that's not it. In this lesson, let us look at how to make adjectives out of verbs.

Again, "adjectives" are a part of speech that modify the nouns (usually) in front of them (i.e. "good" in "good idea" and "awesome" in "awesome music.") And in Korean, not only can descriptive verbs be used as adjectives, or more precisely, but also "action verbs" can used in the form of adjectives.

### Example of descriptive verbs used as adjectives

Nice person (nice + person)
= descriptive verb 좋다 + 사람 = 좋은 사람

Fun game (fun + game)
= descriptive verb 어렵다 + 게임 = 어려운 게임

### Examples of action verbs used as adjectives

노래하는 사람
[no-rae-ha-neun sa-ram]
= 노래하다 (to sing) + 사람 (person)
= (the/a) person who sings

82

**좋아하는 책**
[jo-a-ha-neun chaek]
= 좋아하다 (to like) + 책 (book)
= (the/a) book that I like
→ book who likes ( x )

As you can see above, when verbs are changed into adjectives, the meaning can depend on the context. Your job is to know that the adjective is somehow modifying the noun, and from the overall context, figure out what the adjective part means.

> **Conjugation**
> : Verb stem + -는

**Ex)**
가다 = to go
[ga-da]
Adjective form: 가는
[ga-neun]

자다 = to sleep
[ja-da]
Adjective form: 자는
[ja-neun]

Verb stems ending with ㄹ drop the ㄹ and are followed by -는

**Ex)**
열다 = to open
[yeol-da]
Adjective form: 여는
[yeo-neun]

불다 = to blow
[bul-da]
Adjective form: 부는
[bu-neun]

The adjective part in certain sentences can be longer than just one word.

**Ex)**

좋아하다 = to like; to love
[jo-a-ha-da]

Adjective form: 좋아하는
[jo-a-ha-neun]

좋아하는 책 = a book that I/you/they/someone like(s)

내가(제가) 좋아하는 책 = a book that I like
(Here, "내가 좋아하는" is the adjective part.)

내가(제가) 안 좋아하는 책 = a book that I don't like
(Here, "내가(제가) 안 좋아하는 책" is the adjective part.)

Depending on the context and the use of particles, the entire meaning can change.

Now you know that 좋아하는 is the adjective form of 좋아하다 and that it means "that I/someone like(s)." However, the meaning can change depending on which particle is used.

**Ex)**
좋아하는 사람
[jo-a-ha-neun sa-ram]
= someone that someone likes

= someone I like

민지가 좋아하는 사람
[min-ji-ga jo-a-ha-neun sa-ram]
= someone that Minji likes

민지를 좋아하는 사람
[min-ji-reul jo-a-ha-neun sa-ram]
= someone that likes Minji

*Sample sentences*

1. 이 노래는 제가 좋아하는 노래예요.
[i no-rae-neun je-ga jo-a-ha-neun no-rae-ye-yo.]
= This song is a song that I like.

2. 자주 먹는 한국 음식 있어요?
[ja-ju meok-neun han-guk eum-sik i-sseo-yo?]
= Is there a Korean food that you eat often?

3. 자주 가는 카페 있어요?
[ja-ju ga-neun ka-pe i-sseo-yo?]
= Is there a cafe that you go to often?

4. 요즘 좋아하는 가수는 누구예요?
[yo-jeum jo-a-ha-neun ga-su-neun nu-gu-ye-yo?]
= Which singer do you like these days?

5. 요즘 공부하고 있는 외국어는 일본어예요.
[yo-jeum gong-bu-ha-go it-neun oe-gu-geo-neun il-bo-neo-ye-yo.]
= The foreign language I am studying these days is Japanese.

6. 눈이 오는 날에는 영화 보고 싶어요.
[nu-ni o-neun na-re-neun yeong-hwa bo-go si-peo-yo.]
= On a day when it snows, I want to see a movie.

7. 저기 있는 사람, 아는 사람이에요?
[jeo-gi it-neun sa-ram, a-neun sa-ra-mi-e-yo?]
= That person who is over there, is it someone that you know?

8. 배고픈 사람 (있어요)?
[bae-go-peun sa-ram (i-sseo-yo)?]
= Anybody (who is) hungry?

# Sample dialogue

Track 28

A: 경은 씨, 이 옷, 새로 산 옷이에요?
[gyeong-eun ssi, i ot, sae-ro san o-si-e-yo?]

B: 아니요. 왜요?
[a-ni-yo. wae-yo?]

A: 전에 못 본 옷이라서요.
[jeo-ne mot bon o-si-ra-seo-yo.]

A: Kyeong-eun, these clothes, are they clothes that you've bought recently?

B: No, why?

A: These are clothes that I haven't seen before.

# Exercises for Level 3 Lesson 14

Match the English phrase with the Korean equivalent:

1. someone who someone else likes
= someone I like

a. 민지를 좋아하는 사람
[min-ji-reul jo-a-ha-neun sa-ram]

2. someone that Minji likes

b. 좋아하는 사람
[jo-a-ha-neun sa-ram]

3. someone that likes Minji

c. 민지가 좋아하는 사람
[min-ji-ga jo-a-ha-neun sa-ram]

Translate the following sentences to Korean:

4. Is there a Korean food that you eat often?
* 먹다 = to eat
  [meok-da]
* 자주 = often
  [ja-ju]

(                                                    )

5. Which singer do you like these days?
* 좋아하다 = to like; to love
  [jo-a-ha-da]
* 요즘 = these days
  [yo-jeum]

(                                                    )

Check the
Answers on
p. 174

# LESSON 15

## 그러면, 그럼

Track 29

안녕하세요! Welcome back to another lesson on conjunctions! Today we are introducing a conjunction that means "in that case" or "if so."

그러면 = in that case; if so; then

Do you remember -(으)면? Yes, we introduced it in Level 2 Lesson 23! 만약 -(으)면 or -(으)면 means "if" or "in case." 그러면 is a combination of 그렇다, which means "to be so" and -면.

[geu-reo-myeon]        [geu-reo-ta]

### *A shorter version of* 그러면

In spoken Korean (and often in casual written Korean), instead of saying 그러면, people just use the shortened form, 그럼. Try not to confuse it with 그런, which means "such."

### *Sample sentences*

1. 그러면 이거는 뭐예요?
   [geu-reo-myeon i-geo-neun mwo-ye-yo?]
   = Then, what is THIS?

2. 지금 바빠요? 그러면 언제 안 바빠요?
   [ji-geum ba-ppa-yo? geu-reo-myeon eon-je an ba-ppa-yo?]
   = You're busy now? Then WHEN are you not busy?

3. 한국 음식 좋아해요? 그럼 김밥도 좋아해요?
[han-guk eum-sik jo-a-hae-yo? geu-reom gim-bap-do jo-a-hae-yo?]
= Do you like Korean food? Then do you like kimbap, too?


4. 진짜요? 그럼 이제 어떻게 해요?
[jin-jja-yo? geu-reom i-je eo-tteo-ke hae-yo?]
= Really? If so, what do we do now?


5. 그럼 이거는 어때요?
[geu-reom i-geo-neun eo-ttae-yo?]
= Then how about this one?

# Sample dialogue

1등!

Track 30

A: 너무 졸려요.
[neo-mu jol-lyeo-yo.]

B: 그럼 잠깐 나갔다 와요.
[geu-reom jam-kkan na-gat-da wa-yo.]

A: 그러면 잠깐만 나갔다 올게요.
[geu-reo-myeon jam-kkan-man na-gat-da ol-ge-yo.]

*A: I'm so sleepy.*

*B: Then go outside for a while.*

*A: I will go out just for a while then.*

# Exercises for Level 3 Lesson 15

1. How do you say "in that case," "if so," or "then" in Korean?

(                                    )

1-1. Often used in spoken Korean (and in casual written Korean), what is the shortened form of the previous answer?

(                                    )

Write the following sentences in Korean:

2. You're busy now? Then when are you not busy?
* To be busy = 바쁘다
  [ba-ppeu-da]

(                                    )

3. Then, what is THIS?

(                                    )

Check the
Answers on
p. 174

# *LESSON 16*

## –아/어/여요 (청유형)

안녕하세요! Let's get right into this lesson! Sometimes when you want to do things with other people, you will say things like "let's go," "let's do it," or "let's start." Today in this lesson, let's look at how to say "let's" in Korean.

There are a few different ways to say this in Korean:

1. -**아/어/여요** [polite/plain]

2. -**(으)시죠** [honorific]

3. -**자** [informal]

4. -**(으)ㄹ래요**? [polite/casual]

5. -**(으)실래요**? [polite/formal]

> **Ex)**
>
> **시작하다** = to start; to begin
> [si-ja-ka-da]
> 1. **시작해요.** = Let's start. (plain)
> [si-ja-kae-yo]
> 2. **시작하시죠.** = Let's start. (honorific)
> [si-ja-ka-si-jyo]
> 3. **시작하자.** = Let's start. (informal)
> [si-ja-ka-ja]
> 4. **시작할래요?** = Shall we start? (polite/casual)
> [si-ja-kal-lae-yo?]
> 5. **시작하실래요?** = Shall we start? (polite/formal)
> [si-ja-ka-sil-lae-yo?]

The most frequently used form is number 1, -**아/어/여요**, and we will be focusing on how to understand and use this form to mean "let's." The other forms will be covered through our future lessons.

## -아/어/여요

Yes. This is the same form as the plain present tense, but don't worry. You can tell the difference through context. Let's take a look at a few sample sentences to see how the easily the meaning can be determined.

*Sample Sentences*

1. 저도 서점에 갈 거예요. 같이 가요!
   [jeo-do seo-jeo-me gal geo-ye-yo, ga-chi ga-yo!]
   = I'm going to the bookstore, too. Let's go together!

2. 배 안 고파요? 우리 햄버거 먹어요.
   [bae an go-pa-yo? u-ri haem-beo-geo meo-geo-yo.]
   = Aren't you hungry? Let's eat hamburgers.

3. 지금 두 시예요. 세 시에 여기에서 만나요.
   [ji-geum du si-ye-yo. se si-e yeo-gi-e-seo man-na-yo.]
   = It's two o'clock now. Let's meet here at three o'clock.

4. 저 금요일까지 바빠요. 토요일에 시작해요. 어때요?
   [jeo geu-myo-il-kka-ji ba-ppa-yo. to-yo-i-re si-ja-kae-yo. eo-ttae-yo?]
   = I'll be busy until Friday. Let's start on Saturday. What do you think?

5. 다른 데 가요. 여기 안 좋은 것 같아요.
   [da-reun de ga-yo. yeo-gi an jo-eun geot ga-ta-yo.]
   = Let's go somewhere else. I think this place is not so good.

** Most Korean phrase books out there will teach learners the ending -(으)ㅂ시다. There are some situations that you would be able to use -(으)ㅂ시다 naturally, but not in everyday situations. For example, if you are talking with your close friends, you should never say -(으)ㅂ시다. We will introduce when it is appropriate to use -(으)ㅂ시다 in a future lesson, but for now, please just use -아/어/여요.

# Sample dialogue

**Track 32**

A: 우리 놀이동산 가요.
[u-ri no-ri-dong-san ga-yo.]

B: 저 놀이기구 무서워서 못 타요.
[jeo no-ri-gi-gu mu-seo-wo-seo mot ta-yo.]

A: 그럼 수영장 가요.
[geu-reom su-yeong-jang ga-yo.]

B: 저 수영도 못해요.
[jeo su-yeong-do mo-tae-yo.]

*A: Let's go to the amusement park.*

*B: I cannot go on the rides because I get scared.*

*A: Then let's go to the swimming pool.*

*B: I cannot swim, either.*

# Exercises for Level 3 Lesson 16

1. There are a few different ways to say "let us" or "let's" in Korean. What is the most frequently used way of saying "let's" in Korean?

(                     )

2. Circle the form which is NOT translated as "Let's ..." in Korean:

a) -아/어/여요
b) -(으)시죠
c) -자
d) -(으)ㄴ

3. Circle the sentence which does NOT mean "Let's start" in Korean:
*시작하다 = to start; to begin
 [si-ja-ka-da]

1) 시작해요.
 [si-ja-kae-yo.]
2) 시작하자.
 [si-ja-ka-ja.]
3) 시작하고 싶어요.
 [si-ja-ka-go si-peo-yo.]
4) 시작할래요?
 [si-jak-hal-rae-yo.]

Fill in the blanks with the correct Korean sentence.

4. I'm going to the bookstore, too. Let's go together!
* bookstore = 서점
 [seo-jeom]
저도 서점에 갈 거예요. (               )

5. Aren't you hungry? Let's eat hamburgers.
* hamburger = 햄버거
 [haem-beo-geo]
배 안 고파요? (               )

*Check the Answers on p. 174-175*

위해, 위해서

In this lesson, we are introducing an expression that means "in order to," "in order for," or "for the sake of." The key word in the expression is 위하다.
[wi-ha-da]

**위하다** means "to put forth the effort for something/someone" or "to do something to benefit someone," but it is rarely used as is without being changed to another form.

위해 = 위해서 = in order to/for

**위하다** is rarely used and it is changed to forms like "위해" or "위해서" to mean "in order to", "in order for", or "for the sake of".

위해 = 위하여
위해서 = 위하여서

Sometimes you will see **위하여** instead of **위해**. **위하여** is the original conjugation, but in everyday language, **위하여** is shortened to **위해** (both in written and spoken languages) for the ease of pronunciation.

***Using 위해/위해서 with nouns***

> Noun + -를 위해/위해서
> = in order for + noun = for the sake of + noun

**Ex)**

건강을 위해서
[geon-gang-eul wi-hae-seo]
= for health; for the sake of health; in order to be healthy

회사를 위해서
[hoe-sa-reul wi-hae-seo]
= for the company; for the good of the company

### Using 위해/위해서 *with verbs*

> Verb stem + -기 위해/위해서

**Ex)**

한국에 가기 위해서
[han-gu-ge ga-gi wi-hae-seo]
= in order to go to Korea

일본어를 배우기 위해서
[il-bo-neo-reul bae-u-gi wi-hae-seo]
= in order to learn Japanese

** Please note that using 위해/위해서 in a sentence makes your sentence sound very formal. You will hear/see this a lot in song lyrics, books, and new articles, but not in casual spoken conversations.

*Sample sentences*

1. 수퍼맨은 세계 평화를 위해서 일해요.
[su-peo-mae-neun se-gye pyeong-hwa-reul wi-hae-seo i-rae-yo.]
= Superman works for world peace.

2. 저는 한국에 가기 위해서 열심히 공부했어요.
[jeo-neun han-gu-ge ga-ga wi-hae-seo yeol-si-mi gong-bu-hae-sseo-yo.]
= I studied hard in order to go to Korea.

3. 부모님을 위해서 돈을 모았어요.

[bu-mo-ni-meul wi-hae-seo do-neul mo-a-sseo-yo.]

= I saved up money for my parents.


4. 건강을 위해서 매일 운동하고 있어요.

[geon-gang-eul wi-hae-seo mae-il un-dong-ha-go i-sseo-yo.]

= I am exercising everyday for my health.

# Sample dialogue

Track 34

A: 경은 씨 왜 이렇게 조금 먹어요?
[gyeong-eun ssi wae i-reo-ke jo-geum meo-geo-yo?]

B: 건강을 위해서요.
[geon-gang-eul wi-hae-seo-yo.]

A: 다이어트를 위해서가 아니고요?
[da-i-eo-teu-reul wi-hae-seo-ga a-ni-go-yo?]

A: Kyeong-eun, why are you eating so little?

B: For my health.

A: Not because you are on a diet?

# Exercises for Level 3 Lesson 17

1. How do you say "in order to," "in order for," or "for the sake of" in Korean?

(                                              )

2.  How do you say "for health," "for the sake of health," or "in order to be healthy"?
* health = 건강
      [geon-gang]

(                                              )

3. Write "in order to go to Korea" in Korean.
* to go = 가다
      [ga-da]

(                                              )

4. Translate "I studied hard in order to go to Korea" to Korean.
* to study = 공부하다
      [gong-bu-ha-da]

(                                              )

5. Write the following sentence in Korean: "I am exercising everyday for my health."
* to exercise = 운동하다
        [un-dong-ha-da]

(                                              )

Check the
Answers on
p. 175

# LESSON 18

〜〜〜〜〜

밖에 + 부정형

Track 35

In this lesson, we are looking at how to say "nothing but" or "only" in Korean. We already introduced -만 in Level 2 Lesson 15, but the expression we are introducing in this lesson is different and consists of two parts: "밖에 + negative verb conjugation"
[-man]
[ba-kke]

The way this works is similar to saying "nothing else but" or "do not do anything other than" in English.

밖 = outside; outdoors
밖에 = outside something; other than something; out of the range of something
밖에 + negative verb conjugation = ONLY + verb

> **Construction:**
> Noun + 밖에 + negative conjugation

**Ex)**
콜라(를) 마시다 = to drink cola
[kol-la (-reul) ma-si-da]
콜라밖에 안 마시다 = to only drink cola
[kol-la-ba-kke an ma-si-da]

돈(이) 있다 = to have money
[do-ni it-da]
돈(이) 없다 = to not have money
[do-ni eop-da]
돈밖에 없다 = to have nothing but money, to only have money
[don-ba-kke eop-da]

**Q:** *Are* -만 *and* 밖에 *interchangeable?*

**A:** *The answer is yes and no. Sometimes they are interchangeable, and of course, you have to change the verb in the negative form when you use* 밖에, *but* 밖에 *is generally used more than* -만.

Since you can't use 밖에 with imperative sentences, including -아/어/여 주세요 ("do something for me"), you have to use -만 with imperative sentences (i.e. 이것만 주세요 = Give me this one only.)

In addition, when the verb itself has a negative meaning, -만 is more commonly used than 밖에 (i.e. 저는 닭고기만 싫어해요 = I only hate chicken.)

*Sample sentences*

1.
한국인 친구가 한 명밖에 없어요.
[han-gu-gin chin-gu-ga han myeong-ba-kke eop-sseo-yo.]
= I only have one Korean friend.

한국인 친구는 한 명밖에 없어요.
[han-gu-gin chin-gu-neun han myeong-ba-kke eop-sseo-yo.]
= As for Korean friends, I only have one.

2.
한국어 조금밖에 못해요.
[han-gu-geo jo-geum-ba-kke mo-tae-yo.]
= I can only speak a little bit of Korean.

** Please note that this is not "한국어 조금만 할 수 있어요." When a beginner learner of Korean wants to say "I can speak a little bit of Korean," they usually say "한국어 조금만 할 수 있어요." It is not too big of a problem, and people will understand you, but if you want to sound more natural, please say "한국어 조금밖에 못해요."

3.

**이것밖에 없어요?**
[i-geot-ba-kke eop-sseo-yo?]
= This is it?

= You only have this?


4.

**우리 고양이는 참치밖에 안 먹어요.**
[u-ri go-yang-i-neun cham-chi-ba-kke an meo-geo-yo.]
= My cat only eats tuna.


5.

**왜 공부밖에 안 해요?**
[wae gong-bu-ba-kke an hae-yo?]
= Why do you only study?

## Sample dialogue

Track 36

A: 현우 씨 현금 있어요?
[hyeo-nu ssi, hyeon-geum i-sseo-yo?]

B: 아, 지금 삼천 원밖에 없어요.
[a, ji-geum sam-cheon won-ba-kke eop-sseo-yo.]

A: 그것밖에 없어요? 음.. 그럼 카드로 계산하세요.
[geu-geot-ba-kke eop-sseo-yo? eum... geu-reom ka-deu-ro gye-sa-na-se-yo.]

B: 네.
[ne.]

A: Hyunwoo, do you have cash?

B: Oh, I only have three thousand won right now.

A: You only have that? Well.. then pay with your card.

B: Alright.

# Exercises for Level 3 Lesson 18

Match the Korean word with their English equivalent:

1. To have nothing but money; to only have money

2. To have money

3. To not have money

a. 돈(이) 없다
[don-(i) eop-da]

b. 돈밖에 없다
[don-ba-kke eop-da]

c. 돈(이) 있다
[don-(i) it-da]

Write the following sentences in Korean:

4. As for Korean friends, I only have one.

\* 한국인 친구 = Korean friend
[han-gu-gin chin-gu]

(                                              )

5. I can only speak a little bit of Korean.

(                                              )

Check the
Answers on
p. 175

# LESSON 19

## 다음에, 후에, 뒤에

There are a few different ways to say "after -ing" in Korean. Through this lesson, we will introduce the three most common ways to say it. These three expressions all share a common structure:

-(으)ㄴ + 다음에

-(으)ㄴ + 후에

-(으)ㄴ + 뒤에

These three all mean "after -ing". Let's look at the key nouns

다음 = next time; next
[da-eum]
(i.e. 다음 주 = next week)

후 = after
[hu]
(i.e. 오후 = afternoon)

뒤 = behind; back
[dwi]
(i.e. 등 뒤 = behind the back)

Using any one of these three words, you can make the structure which means "after -ing". The meaning doesn't change depending on the noun part, so these expressions are interchangeable.

> Verb stem + -(으)ㄴ + 다음(or 후/뒤)에 = after -ing

If you remember from our lessons where we introduced how to conjugate verbs so that they can come before nouns to modify them, the "-(으)ㄴ" makes the verb past tense. Since the "-(으)ㄴ" part indicates that the action has been done, it is already in the past tense form. Before "-(으)ㄴ", you put the verb stem.

**Ex)**

편지를 받다 = to receive a letter
[pyeon-ji-reul bat-da]

편지를 받은 다음에 = after receiving a letter
[pyeon-ji-reul ba-deun da-eu-me]
편지를 받은 후에 = after receiving a letter
[pyeon-ji-reul ba-deun hu-e]
편지를 받은 뒤에 = after receiving a letter
[pyeon-ji-reul ba-deun dwi-e]

집에 가다 = to go home
[ji-be ga-da]

집에 간 다음에 = after going home
[ji-be gan da-eu-me]
집에 간 후에 = after going home
[ji-be gan hu-e]
집에 간 뒤에 = after going home
[ji-be gan dwi-e]

책을 읽다 = to read a book
[chae-geul ik-da]

책을 읽은 다음에 = after reading a book
[chae-geul il-geun da-eu-me]
책을 읽은 후에 = after reading a book
[chae-geul il-geun hu-e]
책을 읽은 뒤에 = after reading a book
[chae-geul il-geun dwi-e]

## Sample sentences

1. **영화 본 다음에 우리 커피 마셔요.**
[yeong-hwa bon da-eu-me u-ri keo-pi ma-syeo-yo.]
= After watching the movie, let's drink coffee.

2. **점심을 먹은 다음에, 도서관에 갔어요.**
[jeom-si-meul meo-geun da-eu-me, do-seo-gwa-ne ga-sseo-yo.]
= After having lunch, I went to the library.

3. **이거 한 다음에 뭐 할 거예요?**
[i-geo han da-eu-me mwo hal geo-ye-yo?]
= After doing this, what are you going to do?

4. **그거요? 이거 한 뒤에 할게요.**
[geu-geo-yo? i-geo han dwi-e hal-ge-yo.]
= That one? I'll do it after I do this.

5. **결정한 후에 연락 주세요.**
[gyeol-jeong-han hu-e yeol-lak ju-se-yo.]
= Contact me after you decide.

# Sample dialogue

Track 38

A: 우리 영화 본 다음에 뭐 해요?
[u-ri yeong-hwa bon da-eu-me mwo hae-yo?]

B: 밥 먹으러 가요.
[bap meo-geu-reo ga-yo.]

A: 밥 먹은 다음에는요?
[bap meo-geun da-eu-me-neun-yo?]

A: What are we doing after watching the movie?

B: We are going to eat.

A: What about after eating?

# Exercises for Level 3 Lesson 19

Translate the following sentences to Korean:

1. After receiving a letter.

\* to receive a letter  =  편지를 받다
[pyeon-ji-reul bat-da]

(                                                    )

2. After reading a book.

\* to read a book  =  책을 읽다
[chae-geul ik-da]

(                                                    )

3. After watching the movie, let's drink coffee.

\* to watch a movie  =  영화 보다
[yeong-hwa bo-da]
\* to drink coffee  =  커피 마시다
[keo-pi ma-si-da]

(                                                    )

4. Contact me after you decide.

\* to decide  =  결정하다
[gyeol-jeong-ha-da]

(                                                    )

5. After doing this, what are you going to do?

(                                                    )

Check the
Answers on
p. 175

# LESSON 20

## -아/어/여도

Track 39 In Level 3 Lesson 12, we introduced the conjunction 그래도, which means "but still"
[geu-rae-do]
or "nevertheless." Today we are introducing a verb ending that means the same thing
as 그래도, but can be used to combine two sentences together.

**-아/어/여도** = **even if, even though**
[-a/eo/yeo-do]

{
**Construction**

- Verb stems ending with the vowel ㅗ or ㅏ are followed by -아도
- Verb stems ending with other vowels are followed by -어도
- Verb stems ending with 하 are followed by -여도
}

**Ex)**

보다 = to see
[bo-da]
→ 보아도 = 봐도 = even if you see; even if you look
   [bo-a-do]   [bwa-do]

울다 = to cry
[ul-da]
→ 울어도 = even if you cry; even though you cry
   [u-reo-do]

공부하다 = to study
[gong-bu-ha-da]
→ 공부해도(= 공부하여도) = even if you study; even though you study
   [gong-bu-hae-do] [gong-bu-ha-yeo-do]

Combining two sentences together

요즘에 바빠요. + 그래도 운동은 하고 있어요.
[yo-jeu-me ba-ppa-yo] + [geu-rae-do un-dong-eun ha-go i-sseo-yo.]
= I'm busy these days. But still, I'm doing some exercise.


→   요즘에 바빠도, 운동은 하고 있어요.

= Even though I'm busy these days, I'm still doing some exercise.


*Sample sentences*


1. 집에 가도, 밥이 없어요.
[ji-be ga-do, ba-bi eop-sseo-yo.]
= Even if I go home, there is no food.


2. 택시를 타도, 시간이 오래 걸려요.
[taek-si-reul ta-do, si-ga-ni o-rae geol-lyeo-yo.]
= Even if I take a taxi, it takes a long time.


3. 석진 씨는 제가 전화를 해도 안 받아요.
[seok-jin ssi-neun je-ga jeo-nwa-reul hae-do an ba-da-yo.]
= Even if I call him, 석진 doesn't answer.


4. 냄새는 이상해도 맛있어요.
[naem-sae-neun i-sang-hae-do ma-si-sseo-yo.]
= Even though the smell is weird, it's tasty.


5. 바빠도 한국에 갈 거예요.
[ba-ppa-do han-gu-ge gal geo-ye-yo.]
= Even if I'm busy, I will go to Korea.

# Sample dialogue

Track 40

A: 불을 켜도 사무실이 어두워요.
[bu-reul kyeo-do sa-mu-si-ri eo-du-wo-yo.]

B: 다 켜도 그래요?
[da kyeo-do geu-rae-yo?]

A: 네. 다 켜도 어두워요.
[ne. da kyeo-do eo-du-wo-yo.]

*A: The office is dark even with the light on.*

*B: Even when you turn all the lights on?*

*A: Yes. It's still dark with all the lights on.*

# Exercises for Level 3 Lesson 20

Write the following phrases or sentences in Korean:

1. Even if you cry; even though you cry
* 울다 = to cry
  [ul-da]

(                                        )

2. Even if you study; even though you study

(                                        )

3. Even if you see; even if you look
* 보다 = to see
  [bo-da]

(                                        )

4. Even if I take a taxi, it takes a long time.
* 택시를 타다 = to take a taxi
  [taek-si-reul ta-da]

(                                        )

5. Even if I go home, there is no food.
* 집에 가다 = to go home
  [ji-be ga-da]

(                                        )

Check the
Answers on
p. 175

*Things to Do in Korea*
## Board Game Cafes (보드 게임 카페)

~~~~~~~~

*Finding ways to entertain or pass the time with your 친구 (friends) and 가족 (family) in Korea isn't very difficult, especially with the multitude of 방s (rooms) on every street that are there for just that purpose. A 노래방, or singing room, is a super popular choice of entertainment for everyone. Then there is, of course, the PC방, where you and yours can play PC games to your heart's content for a small hourly fee. A DVD방 is smaller and more intimate than a 영화관 (movie theater), especially with a huge collection of movies to choose from and its private rooms that include couches, wide-screen TVs, and surround sound. Then there is the 보드 카페 or 보드 게임 카페 or 보드 카페 게임방... whatever you choose to call it, it's a board game cafe/room.*

*Although the 보드 카페 fad peaked about 5-6 years ago, you can still find a good number of these cafes around town, especially in places where the nightlife is really hoppin', usually around universities. In Seoul, these areas include 홍대, 강남, 명동, 신촌, 압구정...etc.*

~~~~~~~~

보드카페 *allows you to spend as long as your money will permit you to play your favorite board games. For just 1,000-2,000원 per person for an hour, you and your friends can choose an empty table, and then a waitress/waiter will come and bring you the menu of games! 4-6 people per table works the best, but you can choose from a ton of games, including Risk, Life, MadGab, Clue, UNO, Battleship, SORRY!,...the list seriously seems like it goes on forever. After the game is chosen, tell your waitress/waiter your choice and they will bring the game to your table. The* 직원/종업원 *(employees) are well versed on how to play all of the games, so if there are any questions of discrepancies in how a game is played, just call on your waiter/waitress and he/she will explain it to you. If you're in the middle of a game and become bored or someone is getting too intense and frustrated (everyone has that kind of friend...), you can switch games. In fact, you can switch as many times as you'd like!*

In addition to board games, you can also order 음료 (drinks) and 과자/스낵 (snacks) for purchase. After all, it is a cafe, so what good would it be if you couldn't order coffee? Although, most 보드카페 places are perfectly fine if you decide to bring your own refreshments.

Oh yeah! I forgot to mention that if someone loses, you get to use one of those giant squeaky plastic hammers to whack the loser on the head. :D

Korea's 보드 카페: just one of the many ways to cure boredom and have some fun with your friends or family while you're here.

***

**You're almost finished with Level 3!**
**Keep up the good work! 화이팅~**

# LESSON 21

## -는/은/ㄴ데

Track 41

In this lesson, we are introducing a verb ending that has a very versatile meaning. Let's look at the basic structures first. They are all very similar and all end with -데, but the words that come right before "데" change a bit.

1. -는데 is used after action verbs, after 있다 and 없다, and after -았 or -겠.

2. -은데 is used after descriptive verbs that have a last consonant in the verb stem, except for the consonant ㄹ.

3. -ㄴ데 is used after descriptive verbs that end in a vowel or the consonant ㄹ (in this case, ㄹ is dropped), and after 이다 and 아니다.

**Ex)**

하다 → 하는데
[ha-da]  [ha-neun-de]
있다 → 있는데
[it-da]  [it-neun-de]
먹다 → 먹는데
[meok-da]  [meok-neun-de]
작다 → 작은데
[jak-da]  [ja-geun-de]
좁다 → 좁은데
[jop-da]  [jo-beun-de]
예쁘다 → 예쁜데
[ye-ppeu-da]  [ye-ppeun-de]
멀다 → 먼데
[meol-da]  [meon-de]

*The usages of this ending is very diverse.*

**Usage 1 : Explaining the background or the situation before making a suggestion, a request, or a question.**

**Ex)**
내일 일요일인데, 뭐 할 거예요?
[nae-il i-ryo-i-rin-de, mwo hal geo-ye-yo?]
= It's Sunday tomorrow + (-ㄴ데) + what are you going to do?

**Usage 2 : Explaining the situation before explaining what happened.**

**Ex)**
어제 자고 있었는데, 한국에서 전화가 왔어요.
[eo-je ja-go i-sseot-neun-de, han-gu-ge-seo jeo-nwa-ga wa-sseo-yo.]
= I was sleeping yesterday + (-는데) + I got a phone call from Korea.

**Usage 3 : Showing a result or situation that is contrasted from the previous action or situation.**

**Ex)**
아직 9시인데 벌써 졸려요.
[a-jik a-hop-si-in-de beol-sseo jol-lyeo-yo.]
= It's still 9 o'clock but I am already sleepy.

The second part (after -는데) can be omitted when the meaning can be easily implied.

**Ex)**
준비 많이 했는데(요)...
[jun-bi ma-ni haet-neun-de(-yo)...]
= I prepared a lot, but...

**Usage 4 : Showing surprise or exclamation.**

**Ex)**

멋있는데(요)!
[meo-sit-neun-de(-yo)!]
= Oh, that's cool!

**Usage 5 : Asking a question** (expecting some explanation about a situation or behavior.)

**Ex)**

지금 어디에 있는데(요)?
[ji-geum eo-di-e it-neun-de(-yo)?]
= So where are you now?

**Usage 6 : Expecting an answer or a response.**

**Ex)**

지금(요)? 지금 바쁜데(요).
[ji-geum(-yo)? ji-geum ba-ppeun-de(-yo).]
= Now? I'm busy now, so...

*Sample sentences*

1. 내일 친구 생일인데, 선물을 아직 못 샀어요.
[nae-il chin-gu saeng-i-rin-de, seon-mu-reul a-jik mot sa-sseo-yo.]
= It's my friend's birthday tomorrow, but I haven't been able to buy a present.

2. 이거 일본에서 샀는데, 선물이에요.
[i-geo il-bo-ne-seo sat-neun-de, seon-mu-ri-e-yo.]
= I bought this in Japan, and it's a present for you.

3. 오늘 뉴스에서 봤는데, 그거 진짜예요?
[o-neul nyu-seu-e-seo bwat-neun-de, geu-geo jin-jja-ye-yo?]
= I saw it in the news today. Is that for real?

4. 이거 좋은데요!
[i-geo jo-eun-de-yo!]
= I like this! / This is good!


5. 어? 여기 있었는데.
[eo? yeo-gi i-sseot-neun-de]
= Huh? It was here...


6. 영화 재미있었는데, 무서웠어요.
[yeong-hwa jae-mi-i-sseot-neun-de, mu-seo-wo-sseo-yo.]
= The movie was interesting, but it was scary.


7. 영화 봤는데, 무서웠어요.
[yeong-hwa bwat-neun-de, mu-seo-weo-sseo-yo.]
= I saw a movie, and it was scary.


8. 저 지금 학생인데, 일도 하고 있어요.
[jeo ji-geum hak-saeng-in-de, il-do ha-go i-sseo-yo.]
= I am a student now, but I'm working too.

# Sample dialogue

Track 42

A: 지금 11시인데 아직도 밖이에요?
[ji-geum yeo-ran-si-in-de a-jik-do ba-kki-e-yo?]

B: 이제 집에 갈 거예요.
[i-je ji-be gal geo-ye-yo.]

A: 어두운데 빨리 들어가세요.
[eo-du-un-de ppal-li deu-reo-ga-se-yo.]

*A: It's 11 o'clock. Are you still outside?*

*B: I am going to go home now.*

*A: It's dark. Hurry and go inside.*

# Exercises for Level 2 Lesson 21

1. "Sunday" is "**일요일**" in Korean. How do you say "It's Sunday tomorrow + (-ㄴ데) +
[I-ryo-il]
what are you going to do?"? (Explaining the background or the situation before making a suggestion, a request, or a question.)

(                                              )

2. "To get a phone call" is "**전화가 오다**" in Korean. How do you say "I was sleeping
[jeo-nwa-ga o-da]
yesterday + (-는데) + I got a phone call from Korea."? (Explaining the situation before
explaining what happened)

(                                              )

3. "To be scary" is "**무섭다**" in Korean. How do you say "I saw a movie, and it was
[mu-seop-da]
scary."?

(                                              )

4. "The news" is "**뉴스**" in Korean. How do you say "I saw it in the news today. Is that
[nyu-seu]
for real?"?

(                                              )

5. How do you say "I like this! / This is good!"? (Showing surprise or exclamation)

(                                              )

Check the
Answers on
p. 175

# LESSON 22

## -(으)ㄹ 수도 있어요

Track 43    Let's look at the expression -(으)ㄹ 수도 있다. In fact, this is a combination of two grammar points that we covered in our previous lessons:

1. -(으)ㄹ 수 있다 was introduced in Level 2 Lesson 17 and it means "can, to be able to".
[-(eu)l su-do it-da]

2 -도 was introduced in Level 2 Lesson 13 and it means "also, too".

When these two expressions are combined into -(으)ㄹ 수도 있다, it means "it could...," "it's possible that...," or "it might..." In order to understand why -(으)ㄹ 수도 있다 has such meanings, we first need to take a closer look at the expression -(으)ㄹ 수 있다.

Basically, the word 수 is a noun which, in this particular structure, means "way," "method," or "idea." Therefore, -(으)ㄹ 수 있다 means "there is a way to do...," "there is an idea for doing...," or "there is a possibility for doing..."
[su]

When the meaning of -도, which is "also" or "too", is added to -(으)ㄹ 수 있다, the sentence takes the meaning of "there is also the possibility of..."
[-do]

So, even though sometimes "-(으)ㄹ 수도 있다" COULD mean "to also be able to do something", it usually means "it might," "it could," or "perhaps..."

**Ex)**

**알다** = to know (something/someone)
[al-da]
→ **알 수도 있다** = might know (something/someone)
[al su-do it-da]
→ **제 친구가 알 수도 있어요.** = My friend might know (the person / the thing).
[je chin-gu-ga al su-do i-sseo-yo]

**만나다** = to meet
[man-na-da]
→ **만날 수도 있다** = might meet
[man-nal su-do it-da]
→ **내일 다시 만날 수도 있어요.** = We might meet again tomorrow.
[nae-il da-si man-nal su-do i-sseo-yo]

**작다** = to be small
[jak-da]
→ **작을 수도 있다** = might be small
[ja-geul su-do it-da]
→ **모자가 작을 수도 있어요.** = The hat could be small.
[mo-ja-ga ja-geul su-do i-sseo-yo]


*Sample sentences*


1. **저 내일 올 수도 있어요.**
[jeo nae-il ol su-do i-sseo-yo.]
= I might come here tomorrow.


2. **저 내일 안 올 수도 있어요.**
[jeo nae-il an ol su-do i-sseo-yo.]
= I might not come here tomorrow.


3. **저 내일 못 올 수도 있어요.**
[jeo nae-il mot ol su-do i-sseo-yo.]
= I might not be able to come here tomorrow.


4. **이거 가짜일 수도 있어요.**
[i-geo ga-jja-il su-do i-sseo-yo.]
= This might be fake.


5. **정말 그럴 수도 있어요.**
[jeong-mal geu-reol su-do i-sseo-yo.]
= It might really be so.

# Sample dialogue

Track 44

A: 석진 씨, 저 내일 늦을 수도 있어요.
[seok-jin ssi, jeo nae-il neu-jeul su-do i-sseo-yo.]

B: 왜요?
[wae-yo?]

A: 병원 갈 수도 있어요.
[byeong-won gal su-do i-sseo-yo.]

B: 네. 알겠어요.
[ne. al-ge-sseo-yo.]

A: *Seokjin, I might be late tomorrow.*

B: *Why?*

A: *I might go to the hospital.*

B: *Okay. I got it.*

# Exercises for Level 3 Lesson 22

Write the following words and/or phrases in Korean:

1. Might know (something or someone)

* To know = 알다
  [al-da]

(                                              )

2. Might meet

* To meet = 만나다
  [man-na-da]

(                                              )

3. Might be small

* To be small = 작다
  [jak-da]

(                                              )

4. I might come here tomorrow.

* To come = 오다
  [o-da]

(                                              )

5. This might be fake.

* To be fake = 가짜이다
  [ga-jja-i-da]

(                                              )

*Check the Answers on p. 175*

# LESSON 23

학 (學)

Track 45

Welcome to the 1st Word Builder lesson of TalkToMeInKorean! Word Builder lessons are designed to help you understand how to more efficiently expand your voca-bulary by learning/understanding some common and basic building blocks of Korean words. Many (not all) of the words in the World Builder lessons are based on Chinese characters, otherwise known as 한자, but the meanings of the words can be different from modern-day Chinese characters. You don't have to worry about memorizing the Hanja characters themselves (but if you want to, feel free!) because your goal for these lessons should be to just understand how words are formed and remember the Korean keyword.

Today's keyword is 학.

The Chinese character for this word is 學.

The word 학 is related to "learning," "studying," and "school."

### Sample expressions

학 + 생(person, member, participant) = 학생 (學生) = student
[hak-saeng]

학 + 교(school) = 학교 (學校) = school
[hak-gyo]

학 + 원(house; garden) = 학원 (學院) = private institute
[ha-gwon]

수 (numbers) + 학 = 수학 (數學) = mathematics
[su-hak]

과 (subject; class; species) + 학 = 과학 (科學) = science
[gwa-hak]

어 (word) + 학 = 어학 (語學) = language learning
[eo-hak]

언어 (word+word) + 학 = 언어학 (言語學) = linguistics
[eo-neo-hak]

경제 (economy) + 학 = 경제학 (經濟學) = economics
[gyeong-je-hak]


학 + 자(person) = 학자 (學者) = scholar
[hak-ja]


유 (to stay) + 학 = 유학 (留學) = studying abroad; staying abroad to study
[yu-hak]

유학 (studying abroad) + 생 = 유학생 (留學生) = student studying abroad
[yu-hak-saeng]

전 (to roll, to move) + 학 = 전학 (轉學) = to change schools
[jeo-nak]

전학 (to change schools) + 생 = 전학생 (轉學生) = student who moved to another
[jeo-nak-saeng]
school


학 + 년 (year) = 학년 (學年) = school year
[hang-nyeon]

학 + 기 (period) = 학기 (學期) = semester
[hak-gi]

방 (to release, to let go) + 학 = 방학 (放學) = school vacation
[bang-hak]


장 (recommending) + 학 + 금 (money) = 장학금 (獎學金) = scholarship
[jang-hak-geum]

장 + 학 + 생 = 장학생 (獎學生) = student on scholarship
[jang-hak-saeng]


복 (return) + 학 + 생 = 복학생 (復學生)
[bo-kak-saeng]

= student who has returned to school (usually) after a long break

학 + 습 (acquire) = **학습** (學習) = (formal) learning, studies
[hak-seup]

**한국어 학습** (韓國語 學習) = (formal) Korean learning
[han-gu-geo hak-seup]

독 (alone) + 학 = **독학** (獨學) = self-study, studying by oneself
[do-kak]

# Sample dialogue

Track 46

A: 학교 다니는 거 재밌어요?
[hak-gyo da-ni-neun geo jae-mi-sseo-yo?]

B: 1학년 때만 재밌었어요.
[i-rak-nyeon ttae-man jae-mi-sseo-sseo-yo.]

A: 그럼 지금은요?
[geu-reom ji-geu-meun-yo?]

B: 재미없어요.
[jae-mi-eop-sseo-yo.]

A: Is it fun, attending school?

B: It was only fun in the 1st year.

A: Then how about now?

B: It's not fun.

# Exercises for Level 3 Lesson 23

1. The word (　　) is related to "learning," "studying," and "school."

Write the following words in Korean. All given words are Sino-Korean.

2. Changing schools

* 전 (轉) = to move; to roll
[jeon]

(　　　　　　　　　　　　　　　　　　　　)

3. Scholarship

* 장 (奬) = recommend
[jang]

(　　　　　　　　　　　　　　　　　　　　)

4. Mathematics

* 수 (數) = numbers
[su]

(　　　　　　　　　　　　　　　　　　　　)

5. School year

* 년 (年) = year
[nyeon]

(　　　　　　　　　　　　　　　　　　　　)

Check the
Answers on
p. 175

# LESSON 24

르 불규칙

Track 47  Welcome to another lesson on irregularities. Yay! We are looking at "르"-irregular in this lesson, so let's get started!

르-irregular is applied only to the following three occasions:

Verb stems ending with -르 followed by
+ -아/어/여요
+ -아/어/여서
+ -았/었/였어요

In these cases, 르 is changed to ㄹ and placed at the end of the previous vowel, then you add ONE MORE ㄹ before adding the verb ending.

Even if the verb stem ends with -르, if it is then followed by other endings such as -아/어/여고, -는데, etc., -르 will still stay the same.

**Ex)**
고르다 = to choose; to pick; to select
[go-reu-da]

→ 골라요. = I pick.
[gol-la-yo.]
→ 골라서 = I pick and then; because I pick
[gol-la-seo]
→ 골랐어요. = I picked.
[gol-la-sseo-yo.]

**모르다** = to not know
[mo-reu-da]

→ **몰라요.** = I don't know.
[mol-la-yo.]

→ **몰라서** = because I don't know
[mol-la-seo]

→ **몰랐어요.** = I didn't know.
[mol-la-sseo-yo.]


**빠르다** = to be fast
[ppa-reu-da]

→ **빨라요.** = It is fast.
[ppal-la-yo.]

→ **빨라서** = because it is fast
[ppal-la-seo]

→ **빨랐어요.** = It was fast.
[ppal-la-sseo-yo.]


**자르다** = to cut
[ja-reu-da]

→ **잘라요.** = I cut.
[jal-la-yo.]

→ **잘라서** = I cut and then; because I cut
[jal-la-seo]

→ **잘랐어요.** = I cut.
[jal-la-sseo-yo.]


**기르다** = to grow, to raise
[gi-reu-da]

→ **길러요.** = I grow.
[gil-leo-yo.]

→ **길러서** = I grow and then; because I grow
[gil-leo-seo]

→ **길렀어요.** = I grew.
[gil-leo-sseo-yo.]


*Sample Sentences*

1. **뭐 골랐어요?**
[mwo gol-la-sseo-yo?]
= What did you choose?


2. **저도 몰라요.**
[jeo-do mol-la-yo.]
= I don't know, either.

3. 비행기는 빨라서 좋아요.
[bi-haeng-gi-neun ppal-la-seo jo-a-yo.]
= Planes are good because they are fast. / I like airplanes because they are fast.


4. 누가 케이크 잘랐어요?
[nu-ga ke-i-keu jal-la-sseo-yo?]
= Who cut the cake?


5. 토끼를 5년 동안 길렀어요.
[to-kki-reul o-nyeon dong-an gil-leo-sseo-yo.]
= I had a rabbit as a pet for five years. / I raised a rabbit for five years.

# Sample dialogue

Track 48

A: 경은 씨, 머리 잘랐어요?
[gyeong-eun ssi, meo-ri jal-la-sseo-yo?]

B: 예전에 잘랐어요.
[ye-jeo-ne jal-la-sseo-yo.]

A: 아, 그래요? 몰랐어요.
[a, geu-rae-yo? mol-la-sseo-yo.]

*A: Kyeong-eun, did you cut your hair?*

*B: I cut it some time ago.*

*A: Oh, really? I did not know.*

# Exercises for Level 3 Lesson 24

Translate the following to Korean:

1. [Past tense] I picked (it).

\* 고르다 = to pick; to select
[go-reu-da]

(                                    )

2. What did you choose?

(                                    )

3. [Past tense] I cut (it).

\* 자르다 = to cut
[ja-reu-da]

(                                    )

4. Who cut the cake?

(                                    )

5. Planes are good because they are fast.

\* 빠르다 = to be fast
[ppa-reu-da]

(                                    )

Check the
Answers on
p. 175

# LESSON 25

## –네요

Track 49

As you have seen so far, there are many different types of verb endings in Korean. They all have very specific rules and this one is no exception. If you change a plain sentence to the -네요 form, you indicate that you are expressing your impression, thought, or surprise. You may have heard this ending used in everyday Korean conversation as well as many Korean dramas.

For example, if you just say "맛있어요," it just means that "it is delicious." However, if you say "맛있네요," the sentence expresses that you are impressed or surprised by the taste. While "맛있어요" can mean the same thing when said with the right intonation, it cannot convey the same message when it is written.

**Structure:**
The conjugation is very simple. Just add -네요 after the verb stem or the past tense suffix.

**Ex)**
크다 = to be big (verb stem = 크)
[keu-da]
- 크 + 어요 = 커요 = It's big. (fact)
- 크 + 네요 = 크네요 = (I see that) it is big. / (Oh, I didn't know it was big, but) it is big. (expressing surprise)

잘 어울리다 = to suit someone well; to go well with someone
[jal eo-ul-li-da]
- 잘 어울리 + 어요 = 잘 어울려요. = It looks good on you. (fact)

- 잘 어울리 + 네요 = 잘 어울리네요. = Oh! I find that it looks good on you. (expressing your impression)


맞다 = to be correct
[mat-da]
- 맞 + 아요 = 맞아요 = It's correct. (fact)

- 맞 + 네요 = 맞네요 = I see that it's correct! (Finding out a fact for the first time.)


*Sample Sentences*


1. 여기 있네요!
   [yeo-gi it-ne-yo!]
= Oh, here it is!


2. 이 드라마 재미있네요.
   [i deu-ra-ma jae-mi-it-ne-yo.]
= I find this drama fun to watch.


** If you already know that this drama is fun and you are telling someone else that as a fact, you need to say "이 드라마 재미있어요."


3. 별로 안 춥네요.
   [byeol-lo an chup-ne-yo.]
= Well, it's not that cold.


4. 아무도 안 왔네요.
   [a-mu-do an wat-ne-yo.]
= Oh, look. Nobody is here yet.


5. 벌써 11월이네요.
   [beol-sseo si-bi-rwo-ri-ne-yo.]
= Wow, it's already November!

# Sample dialogue

**Track 50**

A: 다음 주가 벌써 크리스마스네요?
[da-eum ju-ga beol-sseo keu-ri-seu-ma-seu-ne-yo?]

B: 그러게요. 일 년이 벌써 다 갔네요.
[geu-reo-ge-yo. il nyeo-ni beol-sseo da gat-ne-yo.]

A: 시간 참 빠르네요.
[si-gan cham ppa-reu-ne-yo.]

A: Next week is already Christmas?

B: That's right. A year has already gone.

A: Time is so fast.

# Exercises for Level 3 Lesson 25

Write the following expressions in Korean:

1. Oh! It looks good on you. (Expressing that you're impressed)

* to suit someone well = 잘 어울리다
[jal eo-ul-li-da]

(                                              )

2. I see that it's correct! (Finding out a fact for the first time)

* To be correct = 맞다
[mat-da]

(                                              )

3. Oh, here it is.

* Here = 여기
[yeo-gi]

(                                              )

4. Well, it's not that cold.

* To be cold = 춥다
[chup-da]

(                                              )

5. Wow, it's already November.

* November = 11월
[si-bi-rwol]

(                                              )

Check the
Answers on
p. 176

# LESSON 26

## ㄷ 불규칙

Track 51 You have already learned about irregularities which occur with ㅂ and ㄹ. Let's build upon that knowledge and add in irregularities that sometimes happen with ㄷ.

### How ㄷ-irregular works

When the Korean letter ㄷ is the **받침** (the final consonant at the end of a syllable) of
[bat-chim]
a verb stem and is followed by a vowel, ㄷ is changed to ㄹ. Some verbs follow this rule, and some do not.

### Examples of ㄷ irregular verbs

- 듣다 = to listen
  [deut-da]
- 걷다 = to walk
  [geot-da]
- 묻다 = to ask
  [mut-da]
- 싣다 = to load
  [sit-da]
- 깨닫다 = to realize
  [kkae-dat-da]

For these verbs, ㄷ changes to ㄹ when followed by a vowel:

- 듣 + 어서 → 들어서
  [deu-reo-seo]
- 걷 + 어요 → 걸어요
  [geo-reo-yo]

- 묻 + 으면  →  물으면
  [mu-reu-myeon]
- 싣 + 을 거예요  →  실을 거예요
  [si-reul geo-ye-yo]
- 깨닫 + 았어요  →  깨달았어요
  [kkae-da-ra-sseo-yo]


**Examples of verbs that do NOT follow this rule**


- 받다  = to receive
  [bat-da]
- 묻다  = to bury
  [mut-da]
- 닫다  = to close
  [dat-da]
- 믿다  = to believe
  [mit-da]

For these verbs, you keep 받침 as ㄷ, even when it's followed by a vowel:


- 받 + 아서  = 받아서
  [ba-da-seo]
- 묻 + 어요  = 묻어요
  [mu-deo-yo]
- 닫 + 으면  = 닫으면
  [da-deu-myeon]
- 믿 + 어요  = 믿어요
  [mi-deo-yo]


\** Although 묻다 (to ask) and 묻다 (to bury) are spelled the same way, they are conjugated differently and you can only determine the meaning from the context of the sentence.


**Ex)**
I ask.  = 물어요.
I bury.  = 묻어요.

*Usage examples of ㄷ irregular verbs*

1)

듣다 = to listen
[deut-da]
→ 듣고 있어요 = I am listening. (ㄷ doesn't change because -고 begins with a conso-
[deut-go i-sseo-yo]
nant.)

→ 들었어요 = I heard. (ㄷ changes to ㄹ because -었 starts with a vowel.)
[deu-reo-sseo-yo]

2)

걷다 = to walk
[geot-da]
→ 걷는 것 좋아해요 = I like walking. (ㄷ doesn't change because -는 starts with a
[geot-neun geot jo-a-hae-yo]
consonant.)

→ 한 시간 걸었어요 = I walked for an hour. (ㄷ changes to ㄹ because -었 starts with
[han si-gan geo-reo-sseo-yo]
a vowel.)

*Sample Sentences*

1. 어디에서 들었어요?
[eo-di-e-seo deu-reo-sseo-yo?]
= Where did you hear that?

2. 많이 걸었는데, 안 피곤해요.
[ma-ni geo-reot-neun-de, an pi-go-nae-yo.]
= I walked a lot, but I am not tired.

3. 그 이야기를 믿어요?
[geu i-ya-gi-reul mi-deo-yo?]
= Do you believe that story?

4. 물어도 대답이 없어요.
[mu-reo-do dae-da-bi eop-sseo-yo.]
= Even if I ask, there is no answer.

# Sample dialogue

Track 52

A: 석진 씨, 오늘 지하철역에서 사무실까지 걸어서 왔어요?
[seok-jin ssi, o-neul ji-ha-cheol-lyeo-ge-seo sa-mu-sil-kka-ji geo-reo-seo wa-sseo-yo?]

B: 네. 팟캐스트 들으면서 걸어서 왔어요.
[ne. pat-kae-seu-teu deu-reu-myeon-seo geo-reo-seo wa-sseo-yo.]

A: 집에 갈 때도 걸어서 역까지 갈 거예요?
[ji-be gal ttae-do geo-reo-seo yeok-kka-ji gal geo-ye-yo?]

B: 네.
[ne.]

A: Seokjin, did you walk from the subway station to the office today?

B: Yes, I walked while listening to the podcast.

A: Are you going to walk to the station when you go home too?

B: Yes.

# Exercises for Level 3 Lesson 26

Match the Korean word with the proper conjugation:

1. 듣다 = to listen → 듣 + 어서
   [deut-da]

2. 걷다 = to walk → 걷 + 어요
   [geot-da]

3. 받다 = to receive → 받 + 아서
   [bat-da]

4. 닫다 = to close → 닫 + 으면
   [dat-da]

5. 깨닫다 = to realize → 깨닫 + 았어요
   [kkae-dat-da]

a. 바라서
   [ba-ra-seo]
b. 받아서
   [ba-da-seo]
c. 다르면
   [da-reu-myeon]
d. 닫으면
   [da-deu-myeon]
e. 걷어서
   [geo-deo-seo]
f. 걸어서
   [geo-reo-seo]
g. 깨닫았어요
   [kkae-da-da-sseo-yo]
h. 깨달았어요
   [Kkae-da-ra-sseo-yo]
i. 들어서
   [deu-reo-seo]
j. 듣어서
   [deu-deo-seo]

6. Write the following sentence in Korean: "Where did you hear that?"

* 듣다 = to hear
   [deut-da]

(                                    )

Check the
Answers on
p. 176

반말 and 존댓말

Back in Level 1 Lesson 1, we briefly explained the two main categories of honorifics used in the Korean language, and so far, the verb endings and various sentence structures you've learned with us have been in the 존댓말 (polite/formal language) [jon·daet·mal] category.  In this lesson, we'd like to introduce 반말, or casual/informal/intimate [ban·mal] language.

Politeness levels are determined by the verb ending. There are three basic verb endings used to express different politeness levels:

Type 1: -ㅂ니다  = the most polite and most formal ending
[-nida]
Type 2: -(아/어/여)요  = the polite, natural, and slightly formal ending
[-(a/eo/yeo)yo]
Type 3: -아/어/여  = the casual, informal, and intimate ending

Types 1 and 2 are fall under the 존댓말 category, and Type 3 goes into the 반말 category.

**When do you use 반말?**

Generally, 반말 is considered to be the most intimate and casual way of speaking with others in Korean. Therefore, it has no formality at all. You can only use 반말 to someone who is younger than you, someone of the same age as you, or (if the other person is older than you) someone with whom you agreed to mutually use 반말.

If you don't know the other person's age or social status, you should not use 반말 in any circumstance. Once you know the other person's age and find out if he or she is younger than you, you can use 반말. However, it is safer, as well as a nice gesture, to ask the person with whom you are speaking with whether you can use 반말 with him/her.

### *Here are some common cases in which you can use 반말*

1. You are much older than the other person and you know for sure that the other person won't be offended if you use 반말.
2. You are older than the other person and you got his or her permission to use 반말.
3. You are of the same age as the other person and you got his or her permission to use 반말.
4. You are in elementary school, middle school, or high school and you know that all your classmates are of the same age as you.
5. You are talking to yourself or writing in a diary/journal.

### *Here are some common cases in which you SHOULD NOT use 반말*

1. You know the other person only through work and not personally.
2. You are older than the other person, but he or she is your business client or customer.
3. You are older than the other person, but you are talking to the person in an official environment such as business meetings, seminars, lessons, etc.
4. You don't know the other person. You just met him/her.
5. You are younger than the other person and you never got permission from him/her that you can use 반말 to him/her.
6. You are the same age as the other person, but you are both adults and you don't know each other that well.
7. You are older than the other person, but he/she is your boss.

8. You are older than the other person, but he or she or the spouse of your older sibling.

9. You are talking to a large group of people or filming a video blog.


### How do you ask for and give permission to speak in 반말?

There are certain expressions that people say to get permission from the other person to use 반말.

If you are the older one:

1. 말 놔도 돼요?
[mal nwa-do dwae-yo?]
= May I speak in 반말 with you?

** 말을 놓다 literally means to "put down the language" or "lower the language."
[ma-reul no-ta]

2. 말 편하게 해도 돼요?
[mal pyeo-na-ge hae-do dwae-yo?]
= May I speak comfortably with you?


If you are the younger one:

1. 말 놓으셔도 돼요.
[mal no-eu-syeo-do dwae-yo.]
= You can speak casually with me.

2. 말 편하게 하셔도 돼요.
[mal pyeo-na-ge ha-syeo-do dwae-yo.]
= You can speak comfortably with me. / You can speak 반말 with me.


If you are of the same age as the other person:

1. 우리 말 놓을까요?
[u-ri mal no-eul-kka-yo?]
= Shall we speak in 반말 to each other?

2. 말 편하게 해도 되죠?
[mal pyeon-ha-ge hae-do doe-jyo?]
= I can talk in 반말 with you, right?


***How to change*** 존댓말 ***to*** 반말

[Present tense]

-아/어/여요 → -아/어/여

-이에요 / -예요 → -이야 / -야

[Past tense]

-았/었/였어요 → -았/었/였어

[Future tense]

-(으)ㄹ 거예요 → -(으)ㄹ 거야

**Ex)**

1. What is this?

  존댓말: 이거 뭐예요?
  [i-geo mwo-ye-yo?]
  반말: 이거 뭐야?
  [i-geo mwo-ya?]

2. I'm going to work tomorrow.

  존댓말: 내일 일할 거예요.
  [nae-il il-hal geo-ye-yo.]
  반말: 내일 일할 거야.
  [nae-il il-hal geo-ya.]

3. I met a friend yesterday.

  존댓말: 어제 친구 만났어요.
  [eo-je chin-gu man-na-sseo-yo.]
  반말: 어제 친구 만났어.
  [eo-je chin-gu man-na-sseo.]

### Addressing people

When you want to politely address someone using 존댓말, you add the word 씨 such as 경은 씨, 현우 씨, 석진 씨, 소연 씨, and 현정 씨. If you are in a business or school setting, you can add the title of the person's job or status after their name, like 경은 선생님, 현우 회장님, etc., to show more formality toward the addressee.

When you speak in 반말, however, you can just say the name of the person without 씨. In order to make the name sound more natural when you are addressing the other person, you need to add 아 or 야 to the end of the name. Names that end WITHOUT a consonant are followed by 야, and names that end WITH a consonant are followed by 아.
[a]

**Ex)**
경은 → 경은아! (Hey Kyeong-eun!)
[gyeong-eu-na!]
현우 → 현우야! (Hey Hyunwoo!)
[hyeo-nu-ya!]


### Speaking in Third Person

When using a person's name while speaking or writing in third person, 이 is added after names that end with a consonant. Therefore, names like 경은 and 석진 are followed by 이.

If 현우 wants to talk about 석진 in a sentence, he says 석진's name as "석진이".

**Ex)**
석진이가 했어. = Seokjin did it.
[seok-ji-ni-ga hae-sseo.]

# Sample dialogue

**Track 53**

A: 경은 누나, 말 편하게 하세요.
[gyeong-eun nu-na, mal pyeo-na-ge ha-se-yo.]

B: 아, 그래도 될까?
[a, geu-rae-do doel-kka?]

A: 네. 그럼요.
[ne. geu-reom-nyo.]

B: 그래, 석진아. 앞으로 말 놓을게.
[geu-rae, seok-ji-na. a-peu-ro mal no-eul-ge.]

A: Kyeong-eun, speak comfortably.

B: Oh, can I?

A: Yes, of course.

B: Ok, Seokjin. I will speak casually from now.

# Exercises for Level 3 Lesson 27

Please change the following statements from 존댓말 (polite language) to 반말 (casual language) and write the English translation.

[jon-daet-mal]   [ban-mal]

1. 안녕하세요.
[an-nyoeng-ha-se-yo.]

Casual language : (                          )

English translation : (                          )

2. 이거 뭐예요?
[i-geo mwo-ye-yo?]

Casual language : (                          )

English translation : (                          )

3. 어제 친구 만났어요.
[eo-je chin-gu man-na-sseo-yo.]

Casual language : (                          )

English translation : (                          )

True or false:

4. If you want to use 반말 (casual language) to people, you have to get permission.
[ban-mal]

a. True

b. False

5. If you are older than the other person, you can use 반말 (casual language) even though you just met him/her.
[ban-mal]

a. True

b. False

Check the
Answers on
p. 176

# LESSON 28

## –자 (반말, 청유형)

Track 54   Since you now know how and when to use **반말**(casual language), you are well-
[ban-mal]
equipped to learn how to make imperative "let us" or "let's" sentences in **반말**.

Normally, for sentences in present and past tense, you can simply drop the suffix
"**-요**" to change it from **존댓말** to **반말**. However, when you want to say "let's do
[jon-daet-mal]
something" in **반말**, you need to use a completely different ending.

> **Structure:**
> Verb stem + -**자**
> [-ja]

**Ex)**

**하다** = to do
[ha-da]
**하 + 자** = **하자** = Let's do it.
[ha-ja]

**공부하다** = to study
[gong-bu-ha-da]
**공부하 + 자** = **공부하자** = Let's study.
[gong-bu-ha-ja]

**하지 말다** = to not do it
[ha-ji mal-da]
**하지 말 + 자** = **하지 말자** = Let's not do it.
[ha-ji mal-ja]

**먹다** = to eat
[meok-da]
**먹 + 자** = **먹자** = Let's eat.
[meok-ja]

*Sample sentences*

1. 내일 보자.
[nae-il bo-ja.]
= Let's meet tomorrow.

= See you tomorrow.

2. 이거 사자.
[i-geo sa-ja.]
= Let's buy this.

3. 우리 내일은 쉬자.
[u-ri nae-i-reun swi-ja.]
= Let's take a day off tomorrow.

4. 같이 가자.
[ga-chi ga-ja.]
= Let's go together.

5. 조금만 더 기다리자.
[jo-geum-man deo gi-da-ri-ja.]
= Let's wait a little longer.

*More Phrases in* 반말

1. 안녕하세요 → 안녕
[an-nyeong-ha-se-yo]    [an-nyeong]

2. 안녕히 가세요 → 안녕 / 잘 가
[an-nyeong-hi ga-se-yo]    [an-nyeong]  [jal ga]

3. 안녕히 계세요 → 안녕 / 잘 있어
[an-nyeong-hi gye-se-yo]    [an-nyeong]  [jal i-sseo]

4. 저 → 나
[jeo]    [na]

5. ~ 씨 / You → 너
[ssi]    [neo]

6. 네 / 예 → 응 / 어
[ne]  [ye]    [eung]  [eo]

7. 아니요 → 아니 / 아니야
[a-ni-yo]    [a-ni]  [a-ni-ya]

# Sample dialogue

**Track 55**

A: 왜 이렇게 안 오지?
[wae i-reo-ke an o-ji?]

B: 그냥 우리 먼저 가자.
[geu-nyang u-ri meon-jeo ga-ja.]

A: 조금만 더 기다려 보자.
[jo-geum-man deo gi-da-ryeo bo-ja.]

A: Why isn't it/he/she coming?

B: Let's just go first.

A: Let's wait just a little more.

# Exercises for Level 3 Lesson 28

Write the following phrases in Korean using 반말 (casual language):
[ban-mal]

1. Let's do it.
* To do = 하다
[ha-da]

(                                    )

2. Let's not do it.
* To not do (something) = 하지 말다
[ha-ji mal-da]

(                                    )

3. Let's buy this.
* To buy = 사다
[sa-da]

(                                    )

4. Let's wait a little longer.
* To wait = 기다리다
[gi-da-ri-da]

(                                    )

5. Let's go together.
* To go = 가다
[ga-da]

(                                    )

Check the
Answers on
p. 176

# LESSON 29

## ㅅ 불규칙

Track 56    Now that you've learned about irregularities with 르, as well as some instances when ㅂ and ㄷ are the 받침 of a verb stem, let's add ㅅ-irregular to your growing knowledge of Korean!

When ㅅ is the 받침 of a verb stem and it is followed by a vowel, the ㅅ is dropped.

**Ex)**

낫다 = to heal; to recover; to be better (in comparison)
[nat-da]
낫 + 아요 (present tense) → 나아요
                                    [na-a-yo]
= It's better.
= Please feel better.


젓다 = to stir (liquid)
[jeot-da]
젓 + 어요 (present tense) → 저어요
                                    [jeo-eo-yo]
= I stir.
= Please stir it.


잇다 = to connect; to link
[it-da]
잇 + 었어요(past tense) → 이었어요
                                  [i-eo-sseo-yo]
= I connected.
= I linked.


짓다 = to build; to compose
[jit-da]
짓 + 었어요 (past tense) → 지었어요
                                   [ji-eo-sseo-yo]
= I built it. / I composed it.

*Sample sentences*

1. 잘 저으세요.
[jal jeo-eu-se-yo.]
= Stir it well.

2. 두 개를 이었어요.
[du gae-reul i-eo-sseo-yo.]
= I connected the two (objects).

3. 이 집을 누가 지었어요?
[i ji-beul nu-ga ji-eo-sseo-yo?]
= Who built this house?

4. 좋은 이름을 지을 거예요.
[jo-eun i-reu-meul ji-eul geo-ye-yo.]
= I'm going to create a good name.

5. 감기 다 나았어요?
[gam-gi da na-a-sseo-yo?]
= Did you recover (completely) from the cold?

Exceptions

There are some verb stems in which the "ㅅ" 받침 is regular, meaning that the ㅅ is not dropped and it stays the same.

**Ex)**

웃다 = to smile; to laugh
[ut-da]
웃어요. = Smile. / I smile. / He laughs. / They laugh.
[u-seo-yo.]

씻다 = to wash
[ssit-da]
씻을 거예요. = I'm going to wash up. / I'm going to wash it.
[ssi-seul geo-ye-yo.]

벗다 = to take (clothes) off
[beot-da]
신발을 벗어 주세요. = Please take your shoes off.
[sin-ba-reul beo-seo ju-se-yo.]

# Sample dialogue

Track 57

A: 어깨가 너무 아파요.
[eo-kkae-ga neo-mu a-pa-yo.]

B: 왜요?
[wae-yo?]

A: 조깅할 때 팔을 너무 열심히 저은 것 같아요.
[jo-ging-hal ttae pa-reul neo-mu yeol-ssi-mi jeo-eun geot ga-ta-yo.]

B: 빨리 나으세요.
[ppal-li na-eu-se-yo.]

*A: My shoulder hurts so much.*

*B: Why?*

*A: I think I swung my arms too hard when I was jogging.*

*(Literal: I think I stirred my arms too hard while jogging.)*

*B: Get better soon.*

# Exercises for Level 3 Lesson 29

Translate the following phrases to Korean:

1. "It's better" or "Please feel better."

\* 낫다 = to heal; to recover; to feel better
   [nat-da]

(                                                              )

2. Who built this house?

\* 짓다 = to build; to compose
   [jit-da]

(                                                              )

3. Stir it well.

\* 젓다 = to stir
   [jeot-da]

(                                                              )

4. I connected the two (objects).

\* 잇다 = to connect
   [it-da]

(                                                              )

5. Please take your shoes off.

\* 벗다 = to take off
   [beot-da]

(                                                              )

Check the
Answers on
p. 176

# *LESSON 30*

~~~~~~~~

실(室)

Track 58 Word Builder lessons are designed to help you understand how to more efficiently expand your vocabulary by learning/understanding some common and basic building blocks of Korean words. Many (not all) of the words in the World Builder lessons are based on Chinese characters, otherwise known as 한자, but the meanings of the
[han-ja]
words can be different from modern-day Chinese characters. You don't have to worry about memorizing the Hanja characters themselves (but if you want to, feel free!) because your goal for these lessons should be to just understand how words are formed and remember the Korean keyword.

Today's keyword is 실.

The Chinese character for 실 is 室.

The word 실 is related to "room."
[sil]

### Sample expressions
화장 (makeup) + 실 (room) = 화장실 (化粧室) = toilet; bathroom
[hwa-jang-sil]
**분장 (扮裝) also means "makeup," but is specific to stage/theater makeup. Therefore, 분장실
(扮裝室) = dressing room; backstage powder room

교 (school, teach) + 실 (room) = 교실 (敎室) = classroom
[gyo-sil]

연습 (practice) + 실 (room) = 연습실 (練習室) = practice room, practice place
[yeon-seup-sil]

대기 (wait) + 실 (room) = 대기실 (待機室) = waiting room
[dae-gi-sil]

회 (meet) 의 (discuss) + 실 (room) = 회의실 (會議室)
[hoe-ui-sil]
= meeting room, conference room

병 (disease) + 실 (room) = 병실 (病室) = hospital room, patient's room
[byeong-sil]

미용 (beauty treatment) + 실 (room) = 미용실 (美容室)
[mi-yong-sil]
= beauty parlor; hairdresser's place

사 (work) + 무 (work, task) + 실 (room) = 사무실 (事務室) = office
[sa-mu-sil]

교 (school, teach) + 무 (work) + 실 (room) = 교무실 (教務室) = teacher's office
[gyo-mu-sil]

실 (room) + 장 (head, leader) = 실장 (室長) = head of the office
[sil-jang]

실 (room) + 내 (inside) = 실내 (室內) = indoors
[sil-lae]

실 (room) + 외 (outside) = 실외 (室外) = outdoors, outside
[si-roe]

# Sample dialogue

Track 59

A: 화장실이 어디예요?
[hwa-jang-si-ri eo-di-ye-yo?]

B: 3학년 8반 교실 옆에 있어요.
[sa-mak-nyeon pal-ban gyo-sil yeo-pe i-sseo-yo.]

A: 아, 네. 감사합니다.
[a, ne. gam-sa-ham-ni-da.]

A: Where is the bathroom?

B: It's next to the 3rd grade, 8th class classroom.

A: Ah, Ok. Thank you.

# Exercises for Level 2 Lesson 30

1. The word (      ) is related to "room".

Write the following words in Korean. All given words are Sino-Korean.

2. Toilet; bathroom

\* 화장 (化粧) = make-up
[hwa-jang]

(                                                    )

3. Classroom

\* 교 (敎) = school; teach
[gyo]

(                                                    )

4. Hospital room; patient's room

\* 병 (病) = disease
[byeong]

(                                                    )

5. Indoors

\* 내 (內) = inside
[nae]

(                                                    )

*Check the
Answers on
p. 176*

*Harvest festival/Korean thanksgiving*
## Chuseok (추석)

~~~~~~~~~~

추석 *(Chuseok) is one of the biggest national holidays in Korea along with 설날 (Lunar New Year) and 단오/ 수릿날 (Spring festival). It is often referred to as the Korean Thanksgiving, and it is during this 3-day holiday that Koreans travel back to their 고향 (hometown) to celebrate together, share stories and 맛있는 음식 (delicious food), and most importantly, to give thanks to their 조상 (ancestors).*

*The 3-day 추석 holiday will be observed September 11-13 this year (2011), with the actual 추석 day falling on September 12. Although Korea officially follows the Gregorian calendar, the date of 추석 is based on the 음력 (lunar calendar), a calendar based on the cycles of the lunar phase. On this calendar, 추석 is always on the 15th day of the 8th month; however, when placed on the Gregorian calendar, the date of 추석 will be different every year. For example, in 2012, 추석 is September 31, which means the 3-day holiday will be September 30-October 1.*

*A little bit of history...*

*추석 was originally known as 한가위 (Hangawi) and still sometimes referred to as such. Although the exact origin of 추석 is unknown, popular belief and history will tell us that 추석 originated from a month-long weaving competition between two teams during the reign of the third king (태종 무열왕) of the Silla Kingdom. The team that wove the most cloth won, and the winning team would be treated to a big feast by the losing team.*

*However, some scholars believe 추석 stems from the shamanistic practice of worshipping/celebrating and giving thanks to the harvest moon and ancestors. Farmers harvested their crops during this time of year, and after their 추수 (harvest), they would give thanks to their ancestors in a ritual of worship/thanks called 차례. By presenting their ancestors in the sky with a table of items from the new harvest, the farmers paid homage to their gracious ancestors that they believe gave them a bountiful harvest so they could spend the winter months warmly and with plenty of food. They would then share their bounty and products of the first harvest with family, friends, and neighbors.*

*The celebration continued under the bright light of the 달 (moon) with a performance of the 강강수월래, or "circle dance", which incorporates singing, dancing, and playing instruments exclusively by the maidens of the town dressed in their most special 한복. During the day, there was also a 씨름 (Korean wrestling) competition to see who was the town's strongest man. You can still witness these traditions during present-day 추석 celebrations as well as a variety of other folk games.*

Current traditions
Nowadays, there's always a mass exodus of Koreans returning to their hometown or village to join their family and to pay their respects. Highways are packed, cross-country bus and train stations are chaotic, and tickets for said buses and trains are absolutely, positively 매진 (sold out).

If you plan to travel anywhere in, out of, or around Korea during the days of 추석, it's a good idea to book your tickets WAY in advance. If this type of traveling chaos makes you uneasy, it might be best to just stay where you are and hide under a blanket until 추석 is over. Another option is, of course, to just stay where you are and enjoy the crowd-less streets and festivities in town.

On the eve of 추석, it is common for families to gather together to make one of the representative foods of the holiday, 송편 (Songpyeon). These half moon-shaped rice cakes are filled with various things like sweet red beans, chestnuts, sesame seeds...etc. The making of 송편 brings everyone together to re-connect with each other and live happily in the moment.

Koreans wake up in the wee hours of the morning on the day of 추석 to perform 차례. This ceremony is not all that dissimilar from the ritual performed in days past. By dressing in traditional 한복 and setting a table with an abundance of foods, with the star of the table usually being freshly harvested rice, the family

gives thanks to their ancestors. They then sit down at the table to enjoy the meal that is representative of their blessings from their ancestors.

During 추석, the family will 성묘. 성묘 is a noun that literally translates to "visit the tomb/graves of one's ancestors". When the family visits the grave site, they remove the weeds and trim plants that have grown around the grave during the summer as well as offer food and drink to their ancestors. This practice is called 벌초 (Beolcho) and is considered an expression of filial piety.

Tips for surviving 추석 if you're a 외국인:
* Double check the operating hours of the stores and restaurants you may possibly want to visit during the holiday. They may or may not be open!
* Find places to go to that are easily accessible by subway to avoid the holiday traffic. Subway stations will be virtually EMPTY and you will be able to grab a seat anywhere you want to.
* For the few days right before 추석, do not visit E-mart, Home Plus, or any grocery-like store for that matter, unless you are an adventure-seeker and enjoy being trampled by 아줌마들 (ajummas).
* The palaces in Seoul, Korean Folk Village, and 남산골 (Namsangol) village have various 추석 activities, and some museums may have 추석 attractions as well!
* If you want to avoid Korea altogether during 추석, you can book a ticket well in advance to get out of the country and go sight-seeing somewhere else for 3 days.

추석 is a very special time for Korea, and if you are given the chance to experience any of the festivities or rituals, do not pass up the opportunity to engulf yourself in traditional Korean culture.

# Answers

## Level 3 Lesson 1

1. 너무
[neo-mu]
2. 너무
[neo-mu]
3. 너무 빨라요.
[neo-mu ppal-la-yo.]
4. 너무 맛있어요.
[neo-mu ma-si-sseo-yo.]
5. 너무 졸려요.
[neo-mu jol-lyeo-yo.]

## Level 3 Lesson 2

1. 어제 친구를 만났고, 영화를 봤어요.
[eo-je chin-gu-reul man-nat-go, yeong-hwa-reul bwa-sseo-yo.]
  or 어제 친구를 만나고, 영화를 봤어요.
[eo-je chin-gu-reul man-na-go, yeong-hwa-reul bwa-sseo-yo.]
2. 내일 영화를 볼 거고, 쇼핑하러 갈 거예요.
[nae-il yeong-hwa-reul bol geo-go, syo-ping-ha-reo gal geo-ye-yo.]
  or 내일 영화를 보고, 쇼핑하러 갈 거예요.
[nae-il yeong-hwa-reul bo-go, syo-ping-ha-reo gal geo-ye-yo.]
3. 만나고 or 만날 거고
[man-na-go] or [man-nal geo-go]
4. 먹고 or 먹었고
[meok-go] or [meo-geot-go]
5. 책 읽고, 공부하고, 운동했어요.
[chaek il-kko, gong-bu-ha-go, un-dong-hae-sseo-yo.]

## Level 3 Lesson 3

1. 앞        a. front
[ap]
2. 위        d. top
[wi]
3. 밑        e. bottom
[mit]
4. 뒤        b. back
[dwi]
5. 옆        c. side
[yeop]
6. 위에서 : 소파 위에서 자고 있어요.
[wi-e-seo]  [so-pa wi-e-seo ja-go i-sseo-yo.]

## Level 3 Lesson 4

1. 볼까요?
[bol-kka-yo?]
2. 팔까요?
[pal-kka-yo?]
3. 올까요 : 내일 비가 올까요?
[ol-kka-yo]  [nae-il bi-ga ol-kka-yo?]
4. 커피 마실까요? 맥주 마실까요?
[keo-pi ma-sil-kka-yo? maek-ju ma-sil-kka-yo?]

5. 내일 영화 볼까요?
[nae-il yeong-hwa bol-kka-yo?]

## Level 3 Lesson 5

1. 쯤
[jjeum]
2. 한 달쯤, 한 달 정도, 약 한 달
[han dal-jjeum], [han dal jeong-do], [yak han dal]
3. 언제쯤 갈 거예요?
[eon-je-jjeum gal geo-ye-yo?]
4. 내일 몇 시쯤 만날까요?
[nae-il myeot si-jjeum man-nal-kka-yo?]
5. 한국에서 2년쯤 살았어요.
[han-gu-ge-seo i-nyeon-jjeum sa-ral-sseo-yo.]

## Level 3 Lesson 6

1. 1) 공부할 거예요.
[gong-bu-hal ge-ye-yo.]
2. 2) 저도 갈게요.
[jeo-do gal-ge-yo.]
3. 2) 친구들 만날 거예요.
[chin-gu-deul man-nal geo-ye-yo.]
4. 지금 어디예요? 지금 나갈게요.
[ji-geum eo-di-ye-yo? ji-geum na-gal-ge-yo.]
5. 그래요? 다시 할게요.
[geu-rae-yo? da-si hal-ge-yo.]

## Level 3 Lesson 7

1. 해서
[hae-seo]
2. 먹어서
[meo-geo-seo]
3. 와서
[wa-seo]
4. c. ~ 에 따라서
[-e tta-ra-seo]
5. a. 예를 들어서
[ye-reul deu-reo-seo]

## Level 3 Lesson 8

1. 비슷하다
[bi-seu-ta-da]
2. 우리는 나이가 같아요.
[u-ri-neun na-i-ga ga-ta-yo.]
3. 이거랑 이거랑 같아요?
[i-geo-rang i-geo-rang ga-ta-yo?]
4. 커피 같아요.
[keo-pi ga-ta-yo]

5. 그 이야기는 거짓말 같아요.
[geu i-ya-gi-neun geo-jit-mal ga-ta-yo.]


## Level 3 Lesson 9

1. I think they told them. / It looks like they

talked.

   b. 이야기한 것 같아요.
[i-ya-gi-han geot ga-ta-yo.]
2. I think they are talking. / They seem to

talk to each

   c. 이야기하는 것 같아요.
[i-ya-gi-ha-neun geot ga-ta-yo.]
3. I think they will talk. / It seems like they

will talk.

  a. 이야기할 것 같아요.
[i-ya-gi-hal geot ga-ta-yo.]
4. 여기 비싼 것 같아요.
[yeo-gi bi-ssan geot ga-ta-yo.]
5. 그런 것 같아요.
[geu-reon geot ga-ta-yo.]


## Level 3 Lesson 10

1. 전에
[jeo-ne]
2. 공부하기 전에
[gong-bu-ha-gi jeo-ne]
3. 돈을 내기 전에
[do-neul nae-gi jeo-ne]
4. 들어오기 전에 노크 하세요.
[deu-reo-o-gi jeo-ne no-keu ha-se-yo.]
5. 사기 전에 잘 생각하세요.
[sa-gi jeo-ne jal saeng-ga-ka-se-yo.]


## Leve 3 Lesson 11

1. 1) 입다
[ip-da]
2. 2) 어려웠어요
[eo-ryeo-wo-sseo-yo]
3. 이거 너무 귀여워요.
[i-geo neo-mu gwi-yeo-wo-yo.]
4. 이 문제는 어려워요.
[i mun-je-neun eo-ryeo-wo-yo.]
5. 서울은 겨울에 정말 추워요.
[seo-u-reun gyeo-eu-re jeong-mal chu-wo-yo.]


## Level 3 Lesson 12

1. 그래도
[geu-rae-do]
2. 노래방에 가야 돼요. 그래도 노래 안 할 거예요.
[no-rae-bang-e ga-ya dwae-yo. geu-rae-do no-rae an hal geo-ye-yo.]

3. 비가 왔어요. 그래도
[bi-ga wa-sseo-yo.] [geu-rae-do]
어제는 비가 왔어요. 그래도 축구를 했어요.
[eo-je-neun bi-ga wa-sseo-yo. geu-rae-do chuk-gu-reul hae-sseo-yo.]
4. 어려워요. 그래도
[eo-ryeo-wo-yo.] [geu-rae-do]
한국어는 어려워요. 그래도 재미있어요.
[han-gu-geo-neun eo-ryeo-wo-yo. geu-rae-do jae-mi-i-sseo-yo.]


## Level 3 Lesson 13

1. 작은
[ja-geun]
2. 비싼
[bi-ssan]
3. 하얀
[ha-yan]
4. 단
[dan]
5. 더 큰 가방 있어요?
[deo keun ga-bang i-sseo-yo?]


## Level 3 Lesson 14

1. someone that someone likes = someone

I like - b. 좋아하는 사람
[jo-a-ha-neun sa-ram]
2. someone that Minji likes - c. 민지가 좋아하는
[min-ji-ga jo-a-ha-neun
사람
sa-ram]
3. someone that likes Minji - a. 민지를 좋아하는
[min-ji-reul jo-a-ha-neun
사람
sa-ram]
4. 자주 먹는 한국 음식 있어요?
[ja-ju meok-neun han-guk eum-sik i-sseo-yo?]
5. 요즘 좋아하는 가수는 누구예요?
[yo-jeum jo-a-ha-neun ga-su-neun nu-gu-ye-yo?]


## Level 3 Lesson 15

1. 그러면
[geu-reo-myeon]
1-1. 그럼
[geu-reom]
2. 지금 바빠요? 그럼 언제 안 바빠요?
[ji-geum ba-ppa-yo? geu-reom eon-je an ba-ppa-yo?]
3. 그러면 이거는 뭐예요?
[geu-reo-myeon i-geo-neun mwo-ye-yo?]


## Level 3 Lesson 16

1. -아/어/여요

2. d) -(으)ㄴ

3. c) 시작하고 싶어요.
[si-jak-ha-go si-peo-yo.]

4. 같이 가요!
[ga-chi ga-yo!]
5. 우리 햄버거 먹어요.
[u-ri haem-beo-geo meo-geo-yo.]

3. 봐도
[bwa-do]
4. 택시를 타도, 시간이 오래 걸려요.
[taek-si-reul ta-do, si-ga-ni o-rae geol-lyeo-yo.]
5. 집에 가도, 밥이 없어요.
[ji-be ga-do, ba-bi eop-sseo-yo.]

## Level 3 Lesson 17

1. 위해; 위해서
[wi-hae] [wi-hae-seo]
2. 건강을 위해서
[geon-gang-eul wi-hae-seo]
3. 한국에 가기 위해서
[han-gu-ge ga-gi wi-hae-seo]
4. (저는) 한국에 가기 위해서 열심히 공부
했어요.
[(jeo-neun) han-gu-ge ga-gi wi-hae-seo yeol-si-mi gong-bu-
hae-sseo-yo.]
5. (저는) 건강을 위해서 매일 운동하고
있어요.
[(jeo-neun) geon-gang-eul wi-hae-seo mae-il un-dong-ha-go
i-sseo-yo.]

## Leve 3 Lesson 21

1. 내일 일요일인데, 뭐 할 거예요?
[nae-il i-ryo-i-rin-de, mwo hal geo-ye-yo?]
2. 어제 자고 있었는데, 한국에서 전화가 왔어요.
[eo-je ja-go i-sseot-neun-de, han-gu-ge-seo jeo-nwa-ga wa-sseo-yo.]
3. 영화 봤는데, 무서웠어요.
[yeong-hwa bwat-neun-de, mu-seo-wo-sseo-yo.]
4. 오늘 뉴스에서 봤는데, 그거 진짜예요?
[o-neul nyu-seu-e-seo bwat-neun-de, geu-geo jin-jja-ye-yo?]
5. 이거 좋은데요!
[i-geo jo-eun-de-yo!]

## Level 3 Lesson 22

1. 알 수도 있다
[al su-do it-da]
2. 만날 수도 있다
[man-nal su-do it-da]
3. 작을 수도 있다
[ja-geul su-do it-da]
4. 저 내일 올 수도 있어요.
[jeo nae-il ol su-do i-sseo-yo.]
5. 이거 가짜일 수도 있어요.
[i-geo ga-jja-il su-do i-sseo-yo.]

## Level 3 Lesson 18

1. To have nothing but money, to only

have money - b. 돈밖에 없다
[don-ba-kke eop-da]
2. To have money - c. 돈(이) 있다
[don-(i) it-da]
3. To not have money - a. 돈(이) 없다
[don-(i) eop-da]
4. 한국인 친구는 한 명 밖에 없어요.
[han-gu-gin chin-gu-neun han myeong ba-kke eop-sseo-yo.]
5. 한국어 조금밖에 못해요.
[han-gu-geo jo-geum-ba-kke mo-tae-yo.]

## Level 3 Lesson 23

1. 학 (學)
[hak]
2. 전학 (轉學)
[jeo-nak]
3. 장학금 (獎學金)
[jang-hak-geum]
4. 수학 (數學)
[su-hak]
5. 학년 (學年)
[hang-nyeon]

## Level 3 Lesson 19

1. 편지를 받은 다음에, 편지를 받은 후에,
[pyeon-ji-reul ba-deun da-eu-me] [pyeon-ji-reul ba-deun hu-e]
편지를 받은 뒤에
[pyeon-ji-reul ba-deun dwi-e]
2. 책을 읽은 다음에, 책을 읽은 후에, 책을
[chae-geul il-geun da-eu-me] [chae-geul il-geun hu-e]
읽은 뒤에
[chae-geul il-geun dwi-e]
3. 영화 본 다음에 우리 커피 마셔요.
[yeong-hwa bon da-eu-me u-ri keo-pi ma-syeo-yo.]
4. 결정한 후에 연락 주세요.
[gyeol-jeong-han hu-e yeon-lak ju-se-yo.]
5. 이거 한 다음에 뭐 할 거예요?
[i-geo han da-eu-me mwo hal geo-ye-yo?]

## Level 3 Lesson 24

1. 골랐어요.
[gol-la-sseo-yo.]
2. 뭐 골랐어요?
[mwo gol-la-sseo-yo?]
3. 잘랐어요.
[jal-la-sseo-yo.]
4. 누가 케이크 잘랐어요?
[nu-ga ke-i-keu jal-la-sseo-yo?]
5. 비행기는 빨라서 좋아요.
[bi-haeng-gi-neun ppal-la-seo jo-a-yo.]

## Level 3 Lesson 20

1. 울어도
[u-reo-do]
2. 공부해도
[gong-bu-hae-do]

## Level 3 Lesson 25

1. 잘 어울리네요.
[jal eo-ul-li-ne-yo]
2. 맞네요.
[mat-ne-yo]
3. 여기 있네요.
[yeo-gi it-ne-yo]
4. 별로 안 춥네요.
[byeol-lo an chup-ne-yo.]
5. 벌써 11월이네요.
[beol-sseo si-bi-rwo-ri-ne-yo.]

## Level 3 Lesson 26

1. 듣다 = to listen → 듣 + 어서 - i. 들어서
[deut-da]
2. 걷다 = to walk → 걷 + 어요 - f. 걸어서
[geot-da]
3. 받다 = to receive → 받 + 아서 - b. 받아서
[bat-da]
4. 닫다 = to close → 닫 + 으면 - d. 닫으면
[dat-da]
5. 깨닫다 = to realize → 깨닫 + 았어요 -
[kkae-dat-da]
   h. 깨달았어요
[Kkae-da-rat-sseo-yo]
5. 어디에서 들었어요?
[eo-di-e-seo deu-reo-sseo-yo?]

## Level 3 Lesson 27

1. 안녕
[an-nyeong]
2. 이거 뭐야?
[i-geo mwo-ya?]
3. 어제 친구 만났어.
[eo-je chin-gu man-na-sseo.]
4. a. True

5. b. False

## Level 3 Lesson 28

1. 하자.
[ha-ja.]
2. 하지 말자.
[ha-ji mal-ja.]
3. 이거 사자.
[i-geo sa-ja.]
4. 조금만 더 기다리자.
[jo-geum-man deo gi-da-ri-ja.]
5. 같이 가자.
[ga-chi ga-ja.]

## Level 3 Lesson 29

1. 나아요
[na-a-yo.]

2. 이 집을 누가 지었어요?
[i ji-beul nu-ga ji-eo-sseo-yo?]
3. 잘 저으세요.
[jal jeo-eu-se-yo.]
4. 두 개를 이었어요.
[du gae-reul i-eo-sseo-yo.]
5. 신발을 벗어 주세요.
[sin-ba-reul beo-seo ju-se-yo.]

## Level 3 Lesson 30

1. 실 (室)
[sil]
2. 화장실 (化粧室)
[hwa-jang-sil]
3. 교실 (敎室)
[gyo-sil]
4. 병실 (病室)
[byeong-sil]
5. 실내 (室內)
[sil-lae]

The CD on the next page contains key
expressions, sample sentences, sample
expressions and sample dialogues from
the book.

You can download the MP3 files from
the CD at http://TalkToMeInKorean.com
as well.